To Angela,

I've found my
babysitter!

The Accidental Optimist

D1363227

Sav

Em Joy!

The Accidental Optimist

A GUIDE TO LIFE

Emily Joy

Published by Eye Books

The Accidental Optimist: A Guide to Life
1st Edition
September 2005

Published by Eye Books Ltd
Colemore Farm,
Colemore Green,
Bridgnorth
Shropshire
WV16 4ST
Tel/fax: +44 (0) 845 450 8870
website: www.eye-books.com

Printed and bond in Great Britain by Bookmarque Ltd

Set in Frutiger and Garamond by Snowbooks
ISBN: 1903070430

British Library Cataloguing in Publication Data
A catalogue record for this book is available from the British Library

"Life is a series of accidents." Tony

accident *aeksident n.* a chance; that which happens.

optimist *op'tim-ist n.* one who follows the doctrine of Leibniz (1646-1716) that this world is the best of all possible worlds.

life *laif* n. a chance

Acknowledgements

My thanks to all those who I cornered to ask for the meaning of life and those poor souls who feature. In particular Terry, Martin, David, Jo, Tony, Nadine, Craig, Paul and Kristin for some great ideas, my Mum for her biological perspective and, grudgingly, my Dad for sending me off to look in the Dictionary. So I must thank the compilers of the *Chambers*, *Oxford* and *Collins* Dictionaries. Generally I started with Chambers, since I'm a Scot whose favourite colour is red, but if I didn't like their definition, I tried the Oxford or Collins. Most quotes were collected direct from source, but I checked the ones I could in the *Oxford Dictionary of Quotations*. Michael Eysenick's *Psychology: An International Perspective* was a suitably impressive (but remarkably readable) tome to check up on my distant memories of psychology lectures and *Philosophy FOR DUMMIES* was a suitably unimpressive (but very informative) tome for one who has never officially studied philosophy. Dorling Kindersley children's non fiction books are fantastic sources for facts on dinosaurs and the beginning of the world. And of course isn't the internet a wonderful source of info and total rubbish?

My thanks must also go to Dan at Eye books for believing in me, and Chris and Vic for their editing input – in particular for actually seeing some potential in the first draft!

Any spelling mistakes, typos or factual errors are entirely my own fault (largely because I haven't let my Dad read it yet).

Special thanks go to my friends, especially Angela, Heather, Heather, Anne, Suzannah and Wendy for looking after my children so I had chance to get this written. And Terry, of course.

This book is dedicated to Pete

Contents

Prologue

Section 1: Climbing The Pyramid

1. Life is Fragile 15
2. Optimism: Another Word for Denial 32
3. All You Need is Love 41
4. Am I Worth It? 54
5. Life Is A Lot Of Questions 62
6. A Beautiful Life 71
7. The Dizzy Heights 83

Section 2: Tumbling Off The Pyramid

8. Back to Basics. 93
9. Life Begins at Home 101
10. Family Life. 112
11. The Value of Life 120
12. Womb With A View 127
13. For Dear Life 133
14. Life Won't Wait. 148
15. Optimists Don't Worry 154
16. Dr. Jones' Double-Glazing 159
17. Life's Too Short 167
18. Your Life in Their Hands 178
19. Life at a Higher Latitude 184

Section 3: So What *Is* Life?

20. Perhaps, Perhaps, Perhaps 195
21. Answers? 203

Prologue

It is a truth universally acknowledged that a married woman in possession of three children, two dogs and a job, must be in want of a good night's sleep – not the meaning of life.

The philosophers of yore sat navel-gazing in their caves, rooms or gardens, undisturbed by small children, the need to make dinner or change a nappy. Hardly any of them married. How can you talk about life without ever living it? At least the great-granddaddy of philosophy, Socrates (469 – 399 B.C.), took himself out into the world (or at least the streets of Athens) and asked passing strangers what they thought. And he had a wife. But show me the historical document that mentions Socrates pushing a screaming baby in a buggy, or that describes a passing stranger glaring disapprovingly at Socrates Jnr. spread-eagled across the pavement, banging his fists and refusing to walk a step further.

And why were the philosophers such pessimists? Take a look at the photos of all these great minds and you'll see what I mean. What a bunch of grumpy old men! (All men – don't get me started). At least Seneca the Stoic was being true to his philosophy. He thought we were all doomed, and would just make ourselves miserable if we thought otherwise.

> *"Try to come to terms with your wishes and reality. We are made angry by dangerously optimistic notions of what the world is like."* Seneca (4 B.C. – 65 A.D.)

Of course if you go around thinking you're doomed, you probably will be, and ultimately poor old Seneca was. Give him his due, he never complained.

Epicurus (341 B.C. – 270 B.C.) was more my sort of philosopher:

> *"Pleasure is the beginning and the end of living happily."*

...but even he doesn't look as if he ever enjoyed himself. Admittedly, I have only seen a picture of Epicurus' statue, and it may not be very easy to pose with a great big grin on your face for the time it takes to be chipped out in marble. The latter -day great thinkers had no excuse with modern photography. Did they have to be so serious to show how intelligent they are? Not just the philosophers – the psychologists too. Would you tell Freud all your problems? Why can't we be clever and smile? Perhaps thinking all those important thoughts requires so much concentration that nothing can be diverted to the twelve muscles round the lips and eyes necessary for a smile. Or perhaps these great minds know the answer, and that's why they're not smiling.

Which is another good reason not to listen to their answers of - I want to listen to those who are smiling.

"Let other pens dwell on guilt and misery." Jane Austen, *Mansfield Park.*

So I looked in the books and on the internet, trying to find a happy intellectual who didn't dwell on guilt and misery, and out of 421 million entries on Google under 'life' and 17 million on the 'Meaning of Life', plus pages and pages of philosophers, scientists, theologians and psychologists, all with their own opinions, I only found one smiler. (Okay, I have too many children, and too little time to have looked up 17 million entries, but I did spend 20 minutes on line with Ella on my knee and half an hour in the library whilst the boys were at a swimming lesson). Anyway, my smiler is...

Abraham Maslow (1908-1970). As a bonus, the good Dr. Maslow was in possession of six siblings, a wife and two children. Excellent, but does he have anything useful to say? Let me see …hmm, not bad. A hierarchy of needs. A simple triangle to explain everything. Not a circle with its complicated mathematical variables and philosophical considerations of beginnings and ends, nor a rhomboid or a double helix, but a triangle. Maslow's hierarchy of needs:

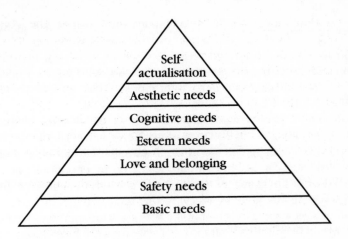

Self-actualisation: Becoming everything that one is capable of becoming.

Aesthetic needs: Beauty, truth, justice, balance and order.

Cognitive needs: Knowledge, understanding and exploration.

Esteem needs: Self-esteem and the respect of others.

Love and belonging: Romantic love, love of your family and friends, being part of a family and a community.

Safety needs: Freedom from fear or anxiety, avoidance of pain, illness, wars or rampaging woolly mammoths.

Basic needs: Our physiological needs such as food, breathing, water, temperature control, sleep, sex.

Maslow's idea was that you couldn't fulfil your higher needs, or your 'growth' needs, until your basic needs were met. These 'lower' needs he termed 'deficiency' needs, implying that you only seek out the oxygen, food, water and sleep that you need, and once satisfied you don't want more. (What rubbish! There's always room for more chocolate).

Oh dear, I haven't made it to the end of the the first chapter without falling out with Dr. Maslow. Never mind. Life would be boring if we all agreed. So in the first section I'm not only going to challenge Dr. Maslow to dig me out of my enormous pile of needs, but I'm going to ask anybody else who might have any tips for life that take my fancy. Asking around might make me a bit of a philosophical slut, but if it was good enough for Socrates, it would be good enough for me. I only want the nice, happy answers though, I don't want to hear that we're all doomed (unless you can put a positive spin on it).

Like this one, from St. Juliana of Norwich (1342-1423):

"All shall be well, and all shall be well, and all manner of thing shall be well."

At last - a woman, and although St. Juliana wasn't exactly smiling, she looks serenely happy (probably because she had no husband or children to contend with). And perhaps she's protesting just a little too much? No, no, I will not let sleep deprivation make me cynical and grumpy. All shall be well (it shall, it shall!) and optimism will triumph over adversity, even for those of us who are not saints. And if it doesn't succeed? Well, it will do better next time.

In the second section, I'm going to apply all this good advice to my own life and see if I could have rescued myself from those moments of optimism failure by realising that everything that has happened to me has happened to someone else, and that I could have learned from others' mistakes rather than having to make them all myself. Having said that, you can't help a chicken to hatch. It has to break its own egg. So I suspect you have to cock-up all by yourself for maximum development. Still, if you'd like to try cheating a little, here's my guide to the series of accidents that make up the triangle of life.

Let's start with the bare necessities *"...look for the bare necessities, the simple bear necessities...".* Sorry. My first film. And you never forget your first.

Section 1

Climbing The Pyramid

1. Life is Fragile

The Bottom Rung: Basic Needs

"Life must eat, metabolise, excrete, breathe, grow, move and reproduce." My Mum (Biology teacher)

"Look for the bear necessities, the simple bear necessities." Baloo the Bear

"To live at all is miracle enough." Mervyn Peake

Prioritise Your Life

Prioritise Your Life! I came across an article whilst sifting through a pile of junk mail and children's drawings looking for my chequebook. Hmmm. It talked about financial investments and aromatherapy facials. Not a single mention of the bare necessities that apply whether you're the Queen, a tree, an amoeba or a bear. Not even a suggestion that food, water, oxygen or sleep might be a priority. Nor any acknowledgment of the need for our other miraculous biological homeostatic mechanisms to be functioning, such as maintaining our pH and temperature within tiny margins. Nor did it suggest that it might be more important to have the smooth disposal of our bodily wastes rather than a smooth face or a very smooth extra percentage point on our interest rates.

Never mind, Dr. Maslow's hierarchy of needs to the rescue. He constructed a list of priorities inspired by his study of monkeys. And Dr. Maslow's monkeys knew their priorities. If they were hungry and thirsty, they would satisfy their thirst before their hunger. Once they'd had a drink, they forgot all about thirst, and could think about their bellies. Bellies full and bladders and bowels emptied, they could then start making more monkeys.

So forget my chequebook, the mortgage, my wrinkles and my cellulite, I'm going to prioritise my life according to a more fundamental analysis than the one offered by today's hyperbolic marketing gurus. Let's start with my favourite basic need. Food. Baloo's favourite bare necessity too, although his preference was for paw-paws, prickly pears, honey and ants. I must say I'd have to be very hungry indeed to eat ants (with or without honey). Give me chocolate any time.

Food

You Can Never Get Enough Chocolate

Chocolate *chok' (a-) lit, n.* preparation in the form of a paste or solid block made from roasted and ground cacao seeds, usually sweetened.

Well if you put it like that, it doesn't sound terribly exciting. So why are there 28 million entries if you Google chocolate? That's 11 million more entries than for the meaning of life! Is chocolate the answer to life the universe and everything?

"He's just adorable," the waitress said. Yes, Art, our nine month old baby, had the capacity to be most adorable. "Would he like a chocolate?"

"That's kind, but no," I answered, a first-time middle class doctor mum with all sorts of nutritional ideals for our precious child.

"No thank you," echoed Danny, Art's doting Dad. "He's never had choc...oh."

Art had already snatched the chocolate from the waitress and was ripping off the shiny wrapper. Why? Why did he know it was something he really, really wanted when he had never had it? Was it the smell? Was it the shiny wrapper? Was it that we had said 'no'?

Our springer spaniel is no better. Bo can sniff out chocolate, double-wrapped inside a box inside a carrier bag sitting amongst ten full carrier bags of the weekly shop. Why? Chocolate is poisonous for dogs (and horses and parrots, apparently). A three stone dog will be poisoned by a half-pound bar of chocolate. A pound of chocolate will give it fits, internal bleeds and heart attacks. But does that put Bo off? No way! Chocolate is poisonous for humans too (if you ate twenty pounds at one sitting – no mean feat, even for me). But look at its benefits!

Chocolate contains over 300 chemicals, including the flavinoids, which lower blood pressure and protect against heart attacks and cancer. Chocolate triggers all the same responses as falling in love, with its secret ingredients such as the psychoactive theobromide, phenyl ethylamine (a cousin of the amphetamines), and small quantities of anadamide (a cannabis-like compound). Chocolate's so good, it's banned in racehorses.

But it's bad for your teeth and will give you spots! Wrong, wrong. Cacao butter is thought to actually protect you from dental plaque and several trials have shown that chocolate doesn't make acne any worse. It will of course make you fat* as it's full of sugar and saturated fats, which we humans are genetically programmed to love. Breast milk, for instance, is full of sugar, so we had a sweet tooth before we even had teeth, and in Stone-age days you might go for a week without food, so you crammed in as many high energy fats and sugars as you possibly could to stave off the forthcoming famine.

Obviously we fat people are just perfect evolutionary survivors from the Stone Age, when the ability to pig out was a lifesaver. Unfortunately, all stuffing yourself does in our times of plenty, is give you diabetes, painful hips and knees and a broken heart (both literally and figuratively).

I have a theory about fat people and thin people. Under stress, thin people lose their appetite, whereas stressed fat people comfort eat. And of course, chocolate is the perfect comfort food, with its melting point being just below human body temperature, so that it melts in the mouth. Ah! Chocolate!

Chocolate covers the whole of Maslow's pyramid:

Basic needs. Eat it or use it to buy other bare necessities (many Central American tribes used cacao liquid or beans as currency) and of course there's 20 reasons why it's better than sex (good when soft, not scared of commitment etc.).

Safety needs. You'll never feel safer than drinking a nice warm mug of hot chocolate.

Love and belonging. Casanova and the Aztec Emperor Montezuma used it as an aphrodisiac and the Aztecs associated cacao with the god of fertility. Today anyone bearing gifts of chocolate will increase their chances of being loved.

Esteem. It makes you feel good.

Cognitive needs. It's full of brain-enhancing chemicals.

Aesthetic needs. It looks and tastes beautiful.

Self-actualisation? Hmmm? I'm sure I'll think of something.

It seems miraculous to me that mankind managed to live without it for thousands of years. The first recorded chocolate beverage was made from the chocolate tree (*Theobroma Cacao*) and drunk by the Aztecs in the fifteenth century, although the Maya Indians were probably using it long before that. Actual chocolate bars didn't make an appearance until the nineteenth century, which means, I regret to say, that chocolate cannot be a panacea for our needs. Perhaps, just perhaps, chocolate is masking unfulfilled needs?

Give up chocolate and get a life? No, no, I can't believe I just said that.

Fat People and Thin People

Lisa (thin person) and I (fat person) were sent to Sierra Leone with Voluntary Service Overseas. Lisa was a nurse tutor and I was a doctor and we shared a house at Serabu Mission Hospital. After sixteen months of chocolate deprivation (me) and three months deprivation (Lisa), we had visitors from the land of chocolate who presented us with two bumper bars of Toblerone. Wow! Now they could come again! My last remaining piece of chocolate (a Minstrel, I remember it well) had been borne off by an army of ants, and my best friend's attempts to fulfil my chocolate needs resulted in a sticky brown package covered in teethmarks, a few shreds of foil and a paper doily that had once been the letter wrapped around the bar of rich dark Bourneville. (And I hope chocolate is poisonous to rats too!) Anyway, this time I was going to nurture my chocolate, so we laid our Toblerone carefully in the fridge, side by side, hoping that eight hours electricity out of twenty-four, would be enough to keep the chocolate under melting point.

I was ENORMOUSLY impressed with myself for making my Toblerone last nearly three days!!!!! Lisa's however, sat in the fridge, with just the tiniest of nibbles from the corner, for over SIX WEEKS.

Every day I would gaze on Lisa's Toblerone and salivate. One night I had been up for hours, repairing the ruptured bowel of a man who had fallen from a palm tree, with the DIY instruction book in one hand and a scalpel in the other. I came home exhausted in the small hours and could bear it no longer. I took my kerosene lamp to the silent fridge, pulled out the chunky triangle from its sleeve, shaved a sliver from the back end with a knife and let it melt in my mouth. Aaah! I covered the evidence carefully with the foil wrapper and replaced the chocolate bar in its cardboard sleeve. Lisa never knew.

Two months passed and over half of Lisa's Toblerone remained. Then SHE STARTED GIVING IT TO THE CHILDREN. I wanted to hurl myself in front of her like a protester in front of a bulldozer in the Amazon forest. Why was she giving her Toblerone away to the African children who had never had chocolate in their lives and were never likely to have it again and probably (possibly) didn't even particularly like it? Surely it was just cruelty, yes cruelty, especially after leaving it there in its full triangular glory to torment me for weeks, to feed it to them when there were others (ME, ME, ME!!!) who would eat the chocolate and be eternally grateful if indeed it was really true that Lisa didn't want it herself (and how could that be?)

I have another theory about fat people and thin people: thin people eat because they have to, but fat people have to eat. (Really inspirational stuff this – STOP PRESS. FAT PEOPLE LIKE FOOD!) Are we fat people just morally deficient? Can enjoying a basic need be morally deficient? Probably. Possibly. Let me tell you about my dog.

A Morally Deficient Dog?

Bo was six weeks old when I first saw her in a freezing barn in the middle of winter, head lost in the foodbowl, little tail wagging, forcing the other puppies 'sharing' her bowl to lick scraps from the edge. Bowl A finished, Bo bounded over to bowl B, where her other four siblings were dining and barged her way in to finish that off too. That's my dog!

Two weeks later we went to collect her. A cluster of adorable springer spaniel pups frolicked in the courtyard. "Aren't they cute?" I sighed. "Which one's Bo?"

"Well…" said the farmer's daughter, embarrassed. "I'm afraid she's got a little, er, fat."

And out rolled a little barrel of fluff and blubber, nearly twice the size of her siblings. Well surprise, surprise, who's been eating my food?

Our other puppy, Rogie, was lean and beautiful. Bo would hoover down a whole bowlful of food and be halfway down Rogie's bowl before Rogie even noticed that dinner had been served. Does that make Bo morally deficient? No. She's a dog. It did make her very unpopular on occasion, e.g.: eating half the Christmas turkey, and it does, of course, make her fat. But not morally deficient.

To make up for my moral deficiency, I once gave up my favourite bottom rung need for a 48 hour sponsored mouth shut, along with my second favourite activity, talking (which bizarrely doesn't appear on the bottom rung, nor anywhere else on Maslow's hierarchy). By the end of the two days I was, not too surprisingly, STARVING – the only time in my life that I've been properly hungry. Westerners (apart from supermodels and other anorexics) are dying of obesity because although we might understand 'peckish', we don't really know what hunger is. In fact we take most of our bottom rung for granted, because generally it's just there without any great effort: food in our pantries, fridges and shops; clean water from our taps; oxygen rich air to breathe; a sun to keep us warm and our marvellous bodies which perform little miracles every second just to keep us functioning without us ever even noticing. But it's an even greater miracle that we exist at all. There was a time when there were no basic needs. When it was minus 273 °C and there was nothing at all.

Heat

The Big Thermostat

Twenty billion years ago it was a bit chilly, but there's nothing like a big bang to warm things up. It was another ten billion years before Earth made an appearance, along with our own personal energy supply, the Sun. Then we had to wait a few million years for our fiery earth-ball to cool down a bit. When it was cool enough to stop all our water boiling off, God could start stirring up his primordial soup. After a few false starts, he perfected the recipe for blue-green algae. God had made the Sun, the seas and (courtesy of his blue-green algae) an ozone layer, so he could keep Experiment Earth at a pretty constant temperature for 350 million years. God even managed to tweak his thermostat to adjust for the occasional obstacle like a meteorite the size of Everest crashing into Earth, which rather disappointingly spoilt his star creation: the dinosaurs.

Then some big-headed bipeds came along and thought they'd get in on the fire thing too. Fire did wonders for man. It gave us heat and light and the courage to leave our caves. It also gave our pretty puny species power over other much more impressive specimens of life with bigger teeth (dragons excepted). No wonder King Louie wanted Mowgli to *give me the power of man's red flower, so I can be like you. Shoo be doo.* Sorry. As I said, my favourite film. Anyway. On with the bare necessities...

Some Like It Hot: Our Internal Thermostat

Hot-blooded animals function best at 37 °C whether you're a polar bear, Marilyn Monroe or a blue tit. We can sneak ourselves a few extra degrees on either side with our fat stores, feathers, fur and shelters. Technology may push that a bit further with fancy central heating, air-conditioning, Gore Tex mountain gear and titanium covered space ships. Leave your Gore Tex jacket behind on Everest and you'll soon drop four or five degrees and your systems will shut down. Throw in a little mosquito in Sierra Leone, and suddenly you have malaria, a temperature of 42.5 °C and, with another couple of degrees, you'll stop functioning permanently.

"Anyone who thinks they are too small to make a difference has never shared a bed with a mosquito." A popular volunteer mantra.

Oh dear! How I hate to be told too much of a good thing is bad for you, but ...

At least too much food will only make you fat, but too much fire is much more destructive. God coped with big meteorites, but can he cope with his unruly monster offspring, man, whose over-consumption is messing up his delicate thermostat in just a few hundred years?

Oxygen

Inspire *in-spir', v.* to breathe in.

Isn't it funny how the things we want the most are bad for you? But the same goes for the things we need the most. If you think chocolate is bad for you, then oxygen is much, much worse. Oxygen feeds the fires, makes cars rust and our cells age, become cancerous and die. A premature baby given 100 percent oxygen will develop all sorts of nasty side effects, like cataracts and brain damage. We can try and protect ourselves by eating lots of antioxidants to prevent the toxic side effects of oxygen. So, eat more chocolate, it will protect you from the air you breathe. Okay, so you might be better to eat more vegetables (although weight for weight the cacoa bean contains ten times more antioxidants than spinach). Plants photosynthesise, so they produce oxygen, so they produce lots of antioxidants to protect themselves. Aren't they clever?

But even though I feel I must have chocolate, I KNOW I must have oxygen.

If you're choking on an organic truffle at the fanciest New York restaurant, Dolce and Gabbana clinging to your fabulous toned curves, just about to sign a multi-million pound advance for your next bestseller, you won't care if it's George Clooney or the ugliest man in the room doing the Heimlich manoeuvre. Nor will you be very interested in that fabulous double chocolate torte that just caught your eye on the sweet menu when you were only supposed to be ordering a starter. Oxygen, oxygen, oxygen. Like most of Maslow's basic needs, you don't miss it till it's gone.

The only time it actually occurred to me to be grateful for oxygen was while scuba diving in the Great Barrier Reef (with a Japanese buddy who spoke no English), too much of a novice to realise I really didn't need so many weights with a thinner, shorter wetsuit. I plunged into the three metre swell, the oxygen regulator bouncing out of my mouth as I torpedoed downwards, panic rather inefficiently wasting any residual circulating oxygen. Would Madam like a lifetime's free Toblerone? No? A diamond ring perhaps? Oxygen, oxygen, oxygen. Anyway, since I'm still here, I would now like to give a belated tribute to those responsible for my oxygen. And the Oscar goes to...blue-green algae!

Blue-green algae were there long before any of us, living five metres down in the oceans, protecting themselves from all that UV radiation that made the Earth's surface even more inhospitable than the moon. Together they photosynthesised, producing oxygen (O_2), which gradually formed ozone (O_3). With the ozone layer protecting Earth from the sun's killer radiation, the rest of us could then creep out of the oceans, first into shallower waters and then onto dry land. And still the blue-green algae photosynthesised, making yet more oxygen for us to breathe. What stars! Inspirational!

But even the blue-green algae couldn't have survived without water, and neither can we.

Water

Our bodies are about 60 percent water (more in babies). We might manage a day, possibly two (if it was cool and we just lay about doing nothing) without it. Oh, how we take it for granted! My hospital in Sierra Leone did have taps, but it was a day for celebration if anything came out of them. Mostly we were rationed to one or two buckets a day for drinking and washing. "God, only one bucket today," I would complain, pitying myself for my traumatic deprivations, when there are millions in this world who would thank their God many times over for that single lovely bucket of water. And I didn't even personally have to carry the big metal bucket the mile from the well. And there *was* a well. And although in the dry season the river dried up to a trickle, it never dried up altogether. In the rainy season you could roll your water barrel under the corrugated iron roof to collect fresh rainwater. But sometimes, in some places, it doesn't rain at all for months and months and months. Sometimes it rains too much and flood water disrupts the sewage systems, then there's not a drop fit to drink.

Excuse me, I'm just going to the loo, which I expect will flush, then I'll have a nice hot bath followed by a long cool glass of water on the rocks.

Talking about going to the loo, there's another, slightly less romantic need...

Excretion

What Goes in Must Come Out

"Kings and philosophers shit and so do ladies." Montaigne (fifteenth century French philosopher)

"Shit happens, but it's not your fault." Seneca (paraphrased a little, perhaps.)

"Shit happens, but then constipation can be very painful." Dr. Em.

Is excretion just a basic function which happens as a side effect of our need for food, oxygen and water, or is it a need in its own right? Well, if you have to do it, it's a need.

If you need to go, you need to go. There's a certain look of bliss, recognised by nurses the world over, on the face of a patient who has opened his bowels after days of difficulty. Children will strain, then preen over their produce in the potty and you must admit there's still a residual sense of satisfaction in a good bowel movement.

Passing urine is also pretty unromantic until you can't do it, due to anatomy (a man with an enlarged prostate), or just circumstance (e.g.: on a long bus journey) and then, oh boy, you want a pee more than sex or even Toblerone! And there's an almost orgasmic sense of relief when you do find that toilet.

Oh look, I've managed to get it back round to chocolate again...

Chocolate Mousse

There's been a lot of poo in my life recently, what with two dogs and three small children. Of course I might have had a lot less trouble if I had followed most of the world and gone for 'Natural Infant Hygiene' – "http://www.naturalinfant.com". No need for nappies, you just respond to their needs, with a little encouraging 'psss, psss' or a 'poo, poo' when you need your little baby to go whilst holding them over a suitable receptacle. Wow! Saves the environment, leaves you totally in tune with your baby and (they say) is no more work in the long run. I am impressed (no, of course I didn't do it!) Clearly I wasn't in tune with anyone.

Art had just turned three. My little boy, fabulous though he was, was sent to try me, and I am no saint. He had been winding me up all Sunday morning. Competitive attention-seeking with his new baby brother, Frankie, who, rather annoyingly for Art, just gurgled and smiled and was generally adorable. Whatever. We'd been up since six and by seven-thirty I'd had enough. Art was looking for trouble. Goading me. Refused to pick up his toys, refused to have breakfast, refused to put his clothes on, refused to go to the toilet. No, no, no! A friend of mine said she never agreed with smacking until she had children. "I never realised that I would actually really, really *want* to smack them!"

Finally Art vanished..."I'm going to the toilet Mummy"...and returned a few minutes later, prancing around with a big blob of poo on his forefinger, laughing and tormenting me with this loaded gun. Look at me, look at me.

"No!" I warned, in the middle of changing baby Frank's nappy (more excretion). "No. No!" Art looked me in the eye, then slowly, purposefully and dramatically he brought the fingerful of poo to his open mouth...

"NOOOOOOOOOOO!" I yelled, launching myself across the room like a slow motion stunt by the hero saving the child from the jaws of death. I rugby tackled my three year old to the floor, grabbing the offending finger and wiping off the...chocolate mousse. Oh.

The next twenty minutes were spent attempting to console my hysterical son.

Sex on the Bottom Rung

People are accused of being basic when they talk about poo, wee and sex. But is sex really that basic? Do we need it to survive?

What is it with psychologists and sex? What is sex doing on the bottom rung? Amoebae for instance manage very well without it. Let's hear it for asexual reproduction. It would save us all a lot of angst. Maybe it's just that psychologists love angst?

It is surely possible to live without sex, although admittedly, the human race can't all live without it indefinitely. And can't you be self-actualised without sex? What about Mother Theresa?

Reproduction, or at least the ability to reproduce, is in the definition of being alive, but we don't all need to reproduce. In fact it's just as well that we don't, as we can't have the entire population exhausted with multiple children. Perhaps that's why bees have a Queen to do all the egg laying, leaving everyone else to do the work? Exhaustion leaves you very selfish – too crushed by the minutiae of life to be worrying about world peace, or the environment. Someone somewhere has to have the energy and inclination to run the country, make miraculous scientific discoveries, write beautiful books, make music, paint pictures, save the world, save souls, save lives etc., etc. Perhaps that's why God invented philosophers, nuns and priests and homosexuality, so at least he'd be guaranteed at least 10 percent of the population available for the above duties? Then there are those who are either too busy self-actualising to find the time to have children. Nothing wrong with that. It just boosts our pool of potential great achievers to 20 percent. And there are those who reproduce, then ignore their offspring and try to get on with their own self-actualisation (trying to write books about priorities, perhaps?)

Of course if you take reproduction out of the equation then you can have loads of sex and still self-actualise. Look at James Bond, for instance (saved the world several times over), or Captain Kirk (saved several worlds), Bill Clinton (would liked to have saved the world) and Ghenghis Khan (who cares about the rest of the world, anyway?)

You'll note that these are all male examples, but for the females of pretty well all species, it's very hard to take reproduction out of the sex equation.

Frequency of sex X *Fertility of participants* = *x (or y) babies*

And don't x (and y are probably worse) babies play havoc with that most longed-for basic need? Sleep.

Sleep, Glorious Sleep

"There was never a child so lovely but his mother was glad to get him to sleep." Ralph Waldo Emerson, (1803-82)

Food might have been my favourite bottom rung need, but since having babies, sleep is now the one that I want. I thought I knew about sleep deprivation as a junior doctor, but at least you weren't on call *every* night.

The Nazis knew a bit about sleep deprivation too, and (supposedly non-Nazi) scientists have done studies on how long we can manage without any sleep. After about three days we start to go psychotic, which was generally thought to be a good time to stop the experiment. They had no such qualms with lab rats, and found that without sleep; they died within two weeks.

Intellectual ability falls by 15 percent if you miss a night's sleep, so after three children, it's a wonder I can even talk. Art, in particular, just didn't want to miss out on any life by wasting it asleep.

Banned from the B&B

Six years after Lisa gave away her Toblerone, she invited us to her baby's christening. Even pregnancy, childbirth and sleep deprivation hadn't driven Lisa to chocolate, but there was no time to dwell on how lean and lovely Lisa had remained when there were so many friends and so much bubbly. After a hard year trying to come to terms with the demands of motherhood, it was great to go to a party and feel like me again, instead of just Art's knackered mummy. Art – always one for a party too – had been a delight all day, and we were bursting with pride at our clever little fellow.

It was 10pm before Danny and I signed into the B&B, rather tipsy and totally exhausted. By rights, Art should have been as exhausted as we were, and after a little story and a song, we tucked him in his travel cot. He never settled. At 11.30pm he was screaming inconsolably. Just like he used to night after bloody night until he was nine months old. So you haven't grown out of it, then? After an hour, it was obvious we weren't going to achieve sleep nirvana, so I carried him downstairs, tiptoeing down the corridor. Tiptoeing was a bit of a waste of time as Art screamed like a Doppler past each of the guest bedrooms. Finally I reached the dark, cold, lounge and shut the door. After an hour of jiggling and pointing out shelves of dodgy ornaments, he dropped into an exhausted sleep. I tiptoed back upstairs, avoiding each creaky step for fear of reawakening the Banshee, then laid him ever so carefully in his cot. Pause.

"Waah, waah, waah!"

Danny took him this time, back down the corridor, past all the guest bedrooms ("Waaaah!!!") and down the stairs (naturally we had the attic room) and into the cold lounge. At four a.m., Danny reappeared, dark-eyed and grumpy and laid the sleeping babe into his cot. Pause.

"Waah, waah waah."

Danny buried his head under the pillow and swore. I started crying. We left Art for a bit, argued a lot, considered divorce (there would be no fighting over who would get custody!) tried songs, tried him in our bed, tried carrying him, swinging him, changing him, feeding him, but nothing worked. Had we not been still under the influence of the fizzy stuff, we would have driven the three hours home right then. We considered strapping him in the car and leaving him there for the rest of the night, but it was a bit cold and surely, *surely*, he had to drop off eventually. Finally after a toss of the coin and another trip past the guest bedrooms ("WaaaAAAH, waaaAAAH, waaaAAAH"), Danny sat with him in the lounge until breakfast. I came downstairs at seven-thirty and there was Art wide awake in the high chair, turning on full beam to both me (don't smile at me like that, mate) and to all the other guests, who smiled sweetly at him and glowered at us.

The owner suggested, ever so nicely, that he had a friend who ran a B&B with big rooms in the middle of a field at the top of a hill somewhere.

Everything depends on your point of view. The last time I had to stay in a hotel there was a baby screaming in the room next door. Okay, so babies scream, and I of all people should know that, so I took positive action rather than moaning. I went for a late swim. But the hotel pool was closed – a small child had pooed in the pool and it would be closed for 24 hours. Shit happens. I went back to my room to find the baby was still screaming. Honestly, people can be so inconsiderate!

Anyway, our own inconsideration had us thrown out. Danny and I drove home in silence, put Art into the furthest bedroom in the house, tucked him into his cot, pigged out on an enormous bar of chocolate and a few glasses of wine, put on our Walkmans and went to bed.

Unfortunately our basic needs aren't interchangeable, so eating more doesn't make up for the loss of sleep (or the loss of love or self-esteem or anything else). More sex might divert you temporarily from having your dinner, but eventually your belly will win and if you are being strangled, then you won't care that you're a bit cold or thirsty or unloved, all you need is oxygen.

So what is the bottom line of the bottom rung? Our bodies are such sensitive, self-correcting machines, with so many needs that it's just amazing any of us survive at all. Life is fragile, even before you start throwing external dangers into the equation.

* Although if anyone has evidence to the contrary, please let me know - www.accidentaloptimist.com

2. Optimism: Another Word for Denial

Safety Second

"He knows not his own strength who has not met adversity." Ben Jonson (1573-1637)

"No pain, no gain". Friedrick Nietzsche (1844-1900), paraphrased a little

Some danger is due entirely to your own stupidity. Some to others' stupidity. Sometimes it's just that others' needs conflict with yours (e.g.: the T-Rex is hungry). And of course some danger is just random accident, some of which can be prepared for, and some that can't. Nothing the dinosaurs did caused that meteorite to crash into earth 65 million years ago, but let's face it, if the dinosaurs were still around, then we wouldn't be. No pain for the dinosaurs, no gain for us. Life is hard. Similarly, illness can hit you at any time. Sometimes you can minimise the chances by doing all the things you should do and not doing any of the things you shouldn't, but the heaviest smoker may not get cancer and the cleanest living monk can still drop dead of a heart attack. Sometimes the most dangerous thing you can do is try to avoid danger.

Too Much Safety is Bad for Your Health

Nietzsche thought we had too much safety, and I'm sure he's right. Even as a small girl, I used to scream with frustration at the story of *The Princess and The Pea* who could still feel the pea underneath 20 mattresses. Oh, for heaven's sake! How was she ever going to survive until her next birthday, never mind managing to produce an heir to the throne? Perhaps I should write the sequel *The Princess and the Pumpkin* and let's just see how she gets on in childbirth. Now, now, optimists aren't mean, but surely we humans do need a little danger to pit ourselves against? Life was meant to be a struggle, and I think we become unhappy if it's just all too easy.

John Morreal, an American philosopher, talks about the first human laughter as originating from the shared relief that danger had passed, inhibiting the flight or fight response and thus increasing trust in the group. So there you go – if there had never been any danger, we would never have started laughing.

Nietzsche would have us live dangerously, overcoming problems and pain to stand, fulfilled, on top of your mountain. But of course, none of us are going to be climbing any mountains without food, water or clothing.

Safety and Our Basic Needs

Our needs are intertwined and can't really be separated into tidy rungs. Safety might be second, but things get pretty dangerous, pretty quickly if you don't meet your basic needs, e.g.: walking on the moon without a spacesuit (survival time – two seconds perhaps), stuck in the desert with no water (survival time – six hours), go on hunger strike (survival time – weeks if water provided, two days if not), driving home from a night shift after no sleep (survival time dependant on other traffic, thus threatening others' safety). Sex is, once again, the exception.

Safe Sex

You are more likely to be endangered having sex than being deprived of it (which is another good reason for taking it off the bottom rung):

a) you're less likely to notice an approaching tiger in the throes of orgasm,

b) pregnancy can be quite dangerous,

c) ditto sexually transmitted disease,

d) we will sacrifice basic needs to get it. e.g.: the male praying mantis, as every biology student knows, can only fulfil his reproductive needs by having his head bitten off by his partner.

Someone Else's Hunger Pangs

Much as the feminist in me cheers Mrs. Praying Mantis, I'm not sure she wins entirely. Who's going to help her with the kids? Eh? I just wouldn't let Danny off that easily. But there are times when you will just have to compromise your safety to fulfil your basic needs. If there was a hungry lion crouching by the last waterhole perhaps, or indeed if the hungry lion was the only thing left to eat.

As well as fighting for your own dinner, you'll have to fight to avoid being someone else's dinner. And there's another reason to keep your mate by your side, because it's very hard to fight off a hungry tiger whilst looking after three children. Keep your mate for tiger bait. (Although unfortunately there's rather more meat on me than Danny, so I'd be the logical choice for a tiger dinner).

Anyway, my only point is that a lot of the danger in the world is due to someone else's hunger pangs. Animals will look after their own safety (e.g.: running away from aforesaid tiger), or the safety of the group (e.g.: fish shoal together to pretend to be one big, angry fish), and generally the safety of their offspring (e.g.: you can't visit the Farne Islands without a hat, to offer some protection from dive-bombing Mummy Terns who assume you're strolling past their nests to eat their eggs).

Plants are pretty stupid. They can't do too much to protect themselves from being eaten by passing herbivores, but they take a much longer-term, and more generous, view than us. They could grow very big, like a tree, so they won't miss a few leaves or fruits, or a lowly lettuce will keep its roots, even if its leaves are eaten, to grow again the next year. In the longer term, evolution might provide a solution, like poisonous berries or thorns, or seeds to be distributed in their consumers' droppings, which is a great, heroic triumph over adversity story. Let's face it, most plants have outlived the dinosaurs (and probably us). Not so stupid.

Other People's Stupidity

You can't get more passive than a plant (Venus flytraps excepted, but they've got to eat, and the flies come to them) and look how successful they are. So why do we have to be so aggressive?

I've led a pretty sheltered life. I was eight or nine before I ever had a proper brush with aggression.

"Are you Catholic or Protestant?" Two teenage girls confronted me.

I would like to say I bravely stood against them, declaring my beliefs, but I didn't understand the question. "Er, I don't know." They didn't believe me. No one, not even a nine year old, could be that ignorant. They grabbed me by the hair and twisted it round their fists and shouted the question at me over and over.

Back home, my mum was brushing out handfuls of hair over the bald patch.

"Mummy," I sobbed. "Am I a Catholic or a Protestant?"

"Well dear, you haven't even been christened."

I'm not sure that that answer would have gone down too well either, but my hair grew back and as random acts of violence go, it was pretty mild. It hasn't burnt a permanent hole in my psyche. In fact, I think I was more upset by the fact I had never been christened, which just goes to show what a sheltered life I've had. Which is probably why I am an optimist. No reason not to be.

Optimists Just Haven't Had Enough Experience

Generally I try to avoid wanton violence or even mild confrontation. I would always lift the dead fly carefully out of the soup and put it on the side of the plate, rather than complain to the waiter and I don't think I've ever taken anything back to a shop. I'm very bad at getting angry. Usually I just get upset, which really doesn't pack much of an intellectual punch with your opponent.

To try and toughen myself up, I used to work an afternoon a week in a drug addiction clinic, which gave me plenty of confrontation skills practice: they wanted their methadone and I didn't want to give it (either because they've already had it, or they haven't picked it up when they should have or they've had so much other stuff, they'd keel over.) Not getting what you want is a common recipe for aggression, necessitating the occasional call to the police, new door or cold compress to a bruised body part, but most of my clients learnt that a barefaced lie with a smile was so much more effective.

My Aunt Fell off the Roof

"I couldn't pick up my prescription last week because my aunt died."

"Oh dear." You just wouldn't believe how many funerals my clients have to attend when they should be in court or picking up their methadone or going to community service.

"My *favourite* aunt, doctor."

"I am sorry. This year you've lost your mum, your dad, your granny, your uncle and now your aunt."

"It's been a bad year."

"And how did your Aunt die?"

"She fell off the roof."

"She fell off the roof?"

"Er, yes."

"Is this the, er, favourite aunt you were telling me about a few months ago. The one in the wheelchair?"

He grinned. Sod it, I gave him his prescription. Creativity should be rewarded. We both knew he wouldn't be getting away with it again.

Life is Hard

"The struggle for existence." Charles Darwin

life *laif n.,* the manner of one's existence. The active part of existence.

I think that means that sitting in front of the telly doesn't count as life. Anyway, to continue my toughening up program, to ensure I was fit to survive life, I went in search of adventure.

You are supposed to feel less safe out of your own environment. Perversely when I arrived in Sierra Leone, I felt very safe. I would go travelling alone, hitching lifts, not worrying if I got stranded because you could just turn up in a village and someone would put you up. I'd never do that back home! You didn't have to worry about the mortgage, there were no telephones, no double-glazing salesmen and children could run around outside and would be looked out for by the rest of the village with no risk of speeding cars. Other dangers could be avoided, like trying not to step on a snake, boiling your water and sleeping under a mosquito net. But you can't stay under a mosquito net all day if you want to eat and find water. If we were sensible, we expatriates took anti-malarials, but the local people who had managed to survive malaria as children had built up a natural immunity. Mother Nature's equilibrium is harsh for some, but generally makes the survivors stronger. Lions and tigers eat the weaker antelope, and if they don't, they die. That's life. Nature is cruel and life is hard.

Man is much crueller than nature. Peaceful Sierra Leone was suddenly plunged into a brutal civil war. The violence, torture and destruction helped no-one and fed no-one. How do you explain that?

Perhaps the explanation's not so hard. People want to climb Neitzsche's mountain (the Nazis, for instance, were fond of Neitzsche), or Tensing's Everest (not caring too much about how many frozen bodies they climb over to get there), or Maslow's pyramid.

Your basic needs are unfilled? You've got no food? Solution: Raid a village and steal some. No sex? Raid a village and help yourself. Feeling unsafe because rebels have burnt down your village? Get yourself a gun and join them and raid another village. No self-esteem? Burn down a village yourself, or point a gun at terrified pregnant woman and feel the power. Love and belonging? Join a band of rebels and egg each other on. Possibly even become their leader. Truth and justice? Convince the outside world that you are doing it to rid your country of corruption. Self-actualisation? Agree to denounce your gun in return for a senior government position in charge of the diamond fields.

So now you are King of your Castle, you can keep all those dirty rascals down on the lower slopes.

No pain, no gain is fine, as long as it's not other people's pain for your gain.

I don't really want to talk about what happened in Sierra Leone, nor any other random awfulness. Because that's what these things are. Random and awful. Planned and awful is worse. The only response is planned and random goodness and kindness. Not hysteria. Not wallowing in how awful it all is, especially when it's somebody else's tragedy. Awfulness always seems so much more awful if you can relate to it, even if it doesn't directly affect you. Which is why we fretted about the few hundred Western tourists who lost their lives on holiday in the Tsunami, rather than the hundreds of thousands of local people. Which is why Sierra Leone hits me harder than Rwanda or the Sudan, and why safe, quiet, middle class Dunblane (the awful thing that happened much closer to home) seemed worse than Hungerford, or even Beslan. It shouldn't be so, but it is. I don't want to think about it, so I don't and I will move on. I want to look on the bright side, I really do. And generally I feel safe, probably because although bad things happen, really bad things haven't happened to me. Yet. Thank God.

Optimism – just another word for denial?

King of the Castle

It's not just human males who damage each other in the game of King of the Castle. Male animals are pretty dangerous to each other, to gain dominance and thus territory (chosen for its ability to provide food and water) and females (it's that unsafe sex again). No wonder Darwin called it the struggle for existence. At least animals don't generally indulge in malice and wanton violence.

Are human atrocities just a response to unfulfilled basic needs? Well, here in the West we no longer have to struggle for existence. We don't have to forage for food, pit ourselves against that woolly mammoth for dinner, or battle with the elements on a daily basis. So what do we do? Pit ourselves against each other?

We have an inborn King of the Castle complex, which is what makes us so interesting, so able to achieve. But please pit yourself against a mountain or the oceans, the theory of relativity, a Latin textbook, or if you really must, an opponent in the boxing ring (I never thought I'd say that, but if you've got to punch someone on the nose, make it a willing competitor), rather than pitting yourself against a passing little girl who'd like to keep her hair, or a pregnant woman who just wants to collect firewood to cook her family's dinner.

We humans can't just sit in our houses all day to avoid any possibility of danger. It wouldn't work, anyway. There are more accidents in the home than on the roads, and how many more would there be if we stayed in all day, going mad with boredom? I can only manage staying in the house until about ten o'clock with my children before I feel like hurling plates across the room. Even God couldn't just sit and do nothing – he had to make a whole universe and a couple of million different life forms, which he must have known would have caused him grief. If we were made in God's image, we humans must also do, or else we die of boredom. Or someone else dies of our boredom.

Freedom from fear and anxiety is what the good Dr. Maslow wanted us to have on his second rung, not for us to wrap ourselves in eiderdown and be totally, boringly safe. Bad things

39

will happen. Even to me. And when they do, we have to deal with them. Life's just too short to worry about it.

"...forget about your troubles and your strife."
Baloo the Bear

So I'll stay in denial, thank you very much.

3. All You Need is Love
(and food, oxygen, sleep ...)

Love *luv, n.* an affection of the mind, caused by that which delights; a sense of underlying oneness

"Love is looking out for someone and knowing they're looking out for you." Terry Langdale, *Moving On*

"Life is Love." Steve (accountant)

What does Dr. Maslow, our resident psychologist have to say about love? (Although I ask reluctantly; psychologists can analyse the life out of anything.)

Maslow defines two types of love: 'D' love, or deficiency love, the love you are given, and 'B' love, the love you give without expectation or the need for reciprocation. 'B' love is the purer more self-actualising love, but you can't give 'B' love unless you have first experienced 'D' love.

D Love

The young Abe Maslow started by studying monkeys with Harry Harlow. Any schoolgirl biologist will remember Harlow's famous series of experiments in 1959: he took baby monkeys from their mothers and provided them with a cloth mummy and a wire mummy, then would frighten them with a mechanical teddy bear beating a drum. (Oh, Dr. Maslow, why didn't you find yourself some nicer friends? Poor little monkeys!) Anyway the monkeys would run to the nice, soft cloth mummy rather than the wire mummy, even if the wire mummy was the one with the bottle of milk. Those motherless babies wanted 'D' love as much as food and it brings a tear to my eye just writing about it. Oh dear, I never used to be the sort of person to cry at films (well apart from *Bambi*, when his mother is shot, and *Old Yeller*, which should have been X-rated), but now every contrived schmaltzy tear-jerker jerks out the tears. It must be having children.

We've all got to have some 'D' love, of some sort, somewhere at some time. Orphanage babies need cuddles as much as food otherwise they lose their appetite, become withdrawn and develop more slowly. Some just die. The more cuddles, the better they do. The effects of their deprivation can be reversed if they are fostered or adopted with love; and the earlier the better. Anyway, that's 'D' love, and I think it belongs on the bottom rung.

B Love

What about 'B' love, the love you give, the purer, more self-actualising love? Well, I'm not sure this is what Maslow had in mind, but it's unrequited love, isn't it? 'B' love – that which is given, not received.

> *"What a grand thing to be loved,*
> *What a grander thing still, to love."* Victor Hugo (1802-1885)

Serial, Unrequited Monogamy

I blame my years of serial, unrequited monogamy on not kissing Terry Swindon. And not liking platform shoes.

> *"Those brown moccasins look fine dear, but how about*
> *something with a bit of a heel?"* My Mum

Despite my mother's best attempts, I remained resolutely flat-shoed and uncool at school.

Generally boys didn't ask girls who beat them at chemistry and didn't wear platform shoes for kisses, but a boy did ask me for a kiss once (oh, yes he did). Okay, so there was a 10:1 boy: girl ratio at the Q.V. Boys' School debate and disco, but he was slightly older and really quite handsome. So here was this nice, good-looking boy who had danced with me all night, saying that I was pretty and that I was lovely and that I was clever and brave to have dared to ask a question, and what did I say? No thanks. Duh?! I went to bed, wishing I had kissed Terry Swindon.

A year later we were back at the Q.V. and this time I was on the debating team. Poor Terry Swindon buried his head in his hands, whilst his pals poked him in the ribs with glee when the only girl to ever spurn a Q.V. boy stood up to speak.

Afterwards, at the disco, the ratio was the same 10:1 but this time, not one boy even asked me for a dance, never mind a kiss. I really should have kissed Terry Swindon. I was only 15 and I was never going to get the chance to be kissed ever again.

Once I had accepted this fact of life, I chugged through the traumatic teenage years without any great angst, interrupted by only one very sweet and chaste love affair with an ecologist (requited at the time) which eased me through the early years of university. After that my lack of glamour took its toll.

A teenager is expected to have terrible make-up and totter about in high heels, but once you reach your twenties and thirties you're expected to have mastered these skills. By the time I thought it might be a good idea to make the transformation into beautiful swan, I was too embarrassed to try. This failing didn't help to convert unrequited to requited on the romantic-love front.

Unrequited love has its advantages though. It is never spoiled by the reality of life, for if world peace is crushed by the minutiae of life then love is a close second casualty. I can honestly say that I've never 'gone off' any of my boyfriends that 'never were', so it's quite nice really. The only one I went off was the one that 'was' which must have some psychological significance. Can I only cope on fantasy island?

Handsome and the Hairdryer

He was a time and a place thing (my lodger, so in my place), devastatingly handsome – no really; very very good-looking – but not nearly as clever as he'd like me to think. He said I was the nicest person he'd ever met, but he was too ashamed by my lack of glamour to be seen out with me (well he was from Newcastle where the girls know how to dress for a bloke). He just couldn't understand why I never wore make-up, or short skirts or high heels or why my ears weren't pierced. But I wasn't much better. It wasn't love, unrequited or otherwise. I accepted his pass out of flattered-ness (as I said v. v. good-looking and a nice Geordie accent), curiosity, and fear that I was about to go to Africa for two years with Voluntary Service Overseas and didn't want to stick myself with an infected needle and die of AIDS a virgin.

Anyway, enough about him. Can't even remember his surname, which says something, although I can remember what he looked like (Timothy Dalton) and our parting exchange. I was clearing out my house, about to rent it for two years while I went to save the world, save my soul, save lives etc. So there I was, a whole house to clear out and clean, whilst he had one small bedroom. Did he help? Even a little bit, a tiny, token gesture bit? Help? I was whizzing about answering phone calls, scrubbing the toilet, fishing out potato peelings from the small gap between the worktop and sink, you know, the usual moving house stress, and he sauntered in, looking gorgeously wet after his shower and asked me if he could borrow my hairdryer.

"What?!! No! I don't have a hairdryer."

"What do you mean, you don't have a hairdryer? Are you a lesbian?"

"No! I just don't have a bloody hairdryer. I've never had a hairdryer."

In my defence, I had short spiky hair at the time and usually dried my hair at the squash courts; I wasn't totally ignorant of the ways of the world. I do now possess a hairdryer, not that I can ever be bothered to use it (and I have even had my ears pierced). Anyway, I was pretty peed off with him. "And I'm unlikely to need one in bloody Africa."

"Oh."

And he left, looking rather bemused. My first, but thankfully not my last, otherwise I would definitely no longer be any sort of an optimist.

Is Your Life Unrequited if Your Love is Unrequited?

Romantic love seems to take an awfully long time to find, then quite often a very short time to lose as your most perfect mate's numerous little failings are slowly revealed as the madness of falling in love wears off. And yet a child will give and receive love instantly (well, at least they do when they are little, I haven't been subjected to teenagers yet) and are apparently unbothered by little failings. The bigger failings, like shouting at them because you're stressed and tired, are quickly forgiven. Why is that? Probably because you don't play hard to get with your baby (even if they are screaming at you), or possibly since the poor little mites can't choose a blonder, slimmer, more immaculately turned-out mummy, they just have to get on with loving you.

Too much choice and too many expectations, that's the problem with romantic love. Either no-one can make their mind up in the first place, imagining there's a better choice round the corner, or they do make their minds up, only to change it a few weeks/months/years/decades down the line, again imagining that 'better' choice.

There's a lot to be said for arranged marriages, with a very rudimentary breakdown to match age, sexuality and (dare I say) some intellectual equality. Then you are presented with your mate and a list of their failings, and they've got a list of yours, so you can sit down and match off on your first meeting. So there's no chemistry on that first date? Well, even God didn't make blue-green algae in a day. No-one's perfect, get over it, then love him or her with all your heart, you're not getting another. Perhaps you could be allowed three tries at a time of your choosing, then divorce would only be granted on proof of lying about your failings. It's got to be better than speed dating, a Las Vegas wedding and a quickie divorce.

But it's not just romantic love that we need. In fact, we probably don't need romantic love at all, as long as we have some love and belonging from other quarters. Indeed, if you spend your early life blinded by sexual love then there's a good chance you'll miss out on a lot of other love: friends, family, work colleagues, all my volunteer friends in Sierra Leone, bonding together against adversity, a joke with a patient, or others at your art class or cheering on your squash team-mates. It's a more general lack of love and belonging in our society that explains half my patient's problems. People move on and leave a void in people's lives and Maslow's third rung needs are sadly left unfulfilled. Fourty percent of marriages crumble, extended families now extend all over the globe (searching for self-actualisation perhaps, but playing havoc with belonging), religion is cast aside in favour of football or popstars (not that I have ever really got to grips with religion, but it does give a great sense of belonging) and even jobs, that once supplied some sort of team of workmates, are all on short-term contracts, or not available at all. So who have they left to go to? Their GP? Okay, so even if you actually like your GP you'll only get ten minutes, so you go to a Counsellor/Homeopathy Practitioner/Chiropracter, or if not actually ill or injured, some sort of Life Coach/Meditation Guru or Aromatherapy Masseuse.

Great – if you have the money, but the people with the problems often don't have the money. Yes you can self-learn, reading books, newspaper articles, magazines and watching videos about all these alternative therapies/ways of living, but that rather misses the point. The whole reason they are successful, is a point of human contact, a focus. Another person focusing solely on you and your problems, making up for our fractured, lonely lives, when all we really need is a bit of community.

Serial Belonging

Belong *bi-long, v.i.* be a member of (a club, family, group etc.)

The people of Sierra Leone had a great sense of belonging, with enormous extended families. Too much belonging perhaps for Western tastes; they had no concept of privacy (nor a word for it). But where I would think, oh how awful, look at all those people crammed in that small house, they would think, how awful, look at that poor lonely woman alone in that big house.

So you had to share your husband with three other wives? Great! Three sisters to help with the childcare and cooking. A husband generally stayed faithful to his wives, so if you were the first wife, exhausted postnatally, he'd sleep with another, until she was pregnant, by which time you'd have your energies back, and back he'd come to you. If you were the youngest, latest wife and your husband was getting a bit past it, nobody frowned too much if you took a love-man on the side. If you happened to get pregnant by your love-man, then all the better: a new baby boosted the status of your elderly husband. A single white woman alone in a house, however, was a total mystery.

"Do you get pickins?" asked Pa George, ex-cook to the Liberian navy, and now reluctant cook to the newly arrived female doctor.

"No, I have no children."

"Do you get man?"

"No, I have no husband."

"Is that why they sent you here?"

Thanks, Pa George.

The Need for Roots

My serial, unrequited monogamy fared no better in Sierra Leone*, but otherwise I had a wonderful time: lots of good friends, both local and expatriate; plenty of excitement and peak experiences. Fitting in was never a problem for me, wherever

I was, from Singapore via Allanbank/Strathedin/New Zealand/ Boldham to Sierra Leone, but now I had reached thirty, I was beginning to get as weary of serial belonging as I was of serial, unrequited monogamy. I longed to put down some roots. So after two-and-a-bit years in Africa, I flew home in time for Christmas at Monikie, my grandparents' home in Strathfarrell, base also to other wayward family members from Japan, Geneva, Dubai and New York.

Monikie provided the one constant in my life, ever since I returned from Singapore, aged three. Apparently I stepped over Twiggy, my grandparents' cairn terrier snoozing in the kitchen doorway, and introduced myself: "Excuse me doggy. Hello Amah, hello Ahcong, hello Aunty Kitchen, I'm Emily."

My mum explained to her parents that Amah and Ahcong meant Grandmother and Grandfather in Singapore, but it actually meant old man and old woman. We never told them. Anyway, Amah and Ahcong, they stayed (Aunty Kit, Amah's sister, remained Aunty Kitchen for a long time too).

Amah and Ahcong had lived in Monikie for fifty years and had been together since they were ten years old. Ahcong was solicitor to half of the Highlands, compere at Burns' Night and Strathfarrell Highland Games, whilst Amah was president of the family and the SWRI. Now that's love and belonging.

So, I've got a great family, just rather far-flung, and at the risk of sounding greedy, just not enough of them. I dreamed of brothers and sisters, to giggle with over midnight feasts, play Monopoly or tennis, or just frolic in the garden. A long-lost twin sister would have done just nicely. I asked my mother why they never had more children, assuming the answer would be along the lines of not wanting to saddle further offspring with the responsibility of matching such perfection, or that they had heartbreakingly suffered a string of disappointments, but had taken comfort in the intelligent, beautiful (okay, a bit porky, but surely that was just a side effect of such loving indulgence?) creature that had sprung from their loins.

"Well we never really planned on you, dear."

Oh. Okay.

How could I complain? At least my parents had produced one child, while it was looking unlikely that I would be replicating any of the Joy genes for eternity. However, once I returned from Sierra Leone, it was clear that it wouldn't matter too much if I personally failed to produce replacements for the human race as most of my friends seemed to have started reproducing whilst I was away. Never mind. I had filled in lots of other bits of my pyramid.

Requited Monogamy

And then I met Danny. Danny was a working-class lad made good, handsome, trim, blond, always immaculately turned out, on the look out for a beautiful, slim and immaculately turned out blonde. But then, if you'd have asked me, I wasn't on the look out for a financial systems analyst who used to have a moustache either. Life is full of surprises.

Danny thought my romantic notion of the big, happy family hilarious. He slept in a shared bed between his brothers, Mick and Rod, born a year either side of him in a two-up two-down terrace (if not quite a cardboard box), forcing Danny into the family toilet at the bottom of the garden for a bit of peace to read. (We have a perfectly large house now, and I still can't get into the toilet). But think of all that cruelty, bickering and appalling sibling rivalries I missed out on. Such a good training ground for life and marriage!

For the Rest of Your life. Roots, Shoots and Stays

Love will keep you warm. It's just as well as it was minus twenty degrees. Sam, my bridesmaid, missed the wedding rehearsal, stranded with Alistair, Danny's best man, and most of the other guests at various points between Drumochter pass and the Slocht, trying to de-ice their windscreens, untouched by their undiluted anti-freeze. So at 6pm, with no bridesmaid or best man, there was me, in Amah's fake fur coat, Danny in fleece and scarf, my Dad, in his duvet anorak (navy), Morag, the minister, in her duvet anorak (red), and Ian, a family friend and Ahcong's partner, playing the organ in his duffle coat and gloves. Dorothy, Ian's wife, wondered if there'd be room for me and my Dad to get past her flower arrangement when I had my dress on. Okay, so I'm a big girl, born to a decent sized dad, but in fact my dress, off the peg in fake lace, made me look really quite streamline (assuming I could survive the next day without thermal underwear). Not that it would matter what I looked like-looking at the weather, there would probably only be about ten people who would be able to get to our wedding anyway.

But life goes on in the most extreme of conditions and love will keep you warm. As will carrying your little bridesmaid over the snow, wearing fleecy trainer bottoms and not a scrap of makeup half an hour before the service, while the bridesmaid's mother dashes back to get herself ready and Alistair's pee was melting the ice in the church toilet bowl. At least my hair was done, blow-dried in the utility room of Amah's hairdresser, up the hill in Strathfarrell, with a wisp of honesty and a bit of MacKenzie tartan ribbon, tonged for good measure. Sam (she made it!) clutched onto me as we slid back down the icy slope, trying not to ruin new hairdos by falling flat on faces. Three days after Christmas with the A9 waist deep in snow, meant the gritters weren't really too concerned about the state of Golf Course Road in Strathfarrell.

Things warmed up on the day itself to minus fourteen degrees. The church filled with bodies' huddling in duffle coats, scarves, fake furs and fleeces. Everybody came! Must have been the excitement, or perhaps carrying little bridesmaids around, but I was toasty warm. Danny said he was warm too. I'd like to put it down to the glow of expectation of marrying such a great catch, but suspect it was all those wee drams into the wee hours, or perhaps the sledging on the golf course that morning? But he was smiling, always a good sign in a groom, and very smart in his kilt. An Englishman, but that's okay. Half the blokes offered him their moral support, and appeared kitted out from the local Highland dress hire. They all looked great, and not one of them cold. Mark, my four year old American cousin, decided he would wear a skirt after all, and looked so sweet that we made him an on the spot page boy. "I liked being a peach boy," he said.

Morag, ever mindful of the shivering bridesmaids, kept the service short and sweet. She had already promised she wouldn't mention the bit about honouring and obeying your husband. Good on you, Morag! We walked down the aisle, man and wife, the congregation following and threw open the church doors to brilliant sunshine and 'AAAGH', possibly a similar facial expression to 'cheese'. All that beautiful sunshine had only managed to notch the thermometer up to minus thirteen. It was a very short photo session. But there's nothing like a bit of adversity to bring out the high spirits, always helped by plenty of bubbly in front of the fire. Once we'd been toasted, Sam and the bridesmaids had been toasted, and I toasted Amah and Ahcong, my perfect example of long life and happiness in marriage, I grabbed a bottle of fizz and made sure everyone was well topped up. Much better than shaking hands.

Perhaps it was the trauma of getting there, or the cold, or the extra fizz, or just that I am biased, but it was the best wedding ever. I looked slim, although had only lost a couple of pounds, which just goes to show it's all psychological. There was a sudden rush of shyness at the bouquet throwing moment. People getting married in their thirties find their friends are either already married, divorced, gay, or have been in relationships so long it would surely not be my place to thrust a bouquet in their arms, much as I would have liked to direct it. So I threw my big bunch of flowers into the crowd and the crowd parted, leaving the splattered bouquet in the middle of a ring of giggling women.

"Oh, for heaven's sake." I picked up my battered, but still beautiful, bunch of flowers and pulled out the golden chrysanthemums, yellow dahlias (and other flowers that I don't know the names of) and handed a couple of flowers to Sam, to Amah, to Alistair, to cousin Sophie and anybody else who was passing. Then we all did a Strip the Willow.

Danny and I ceilidhed until the last guest had gone either to their room, the bus back to Strathfarrell, or the bar. They say you miss the best party of your life, your funeral, so it seemed a bit of a waste to miss most of your second best. The clock passed midnight and I didn't change back into a pumpkin, remaining what I consider to be the most glamorous I have ever looked (albeit after rather too much fizz, I was probably no longer the best judge).

"Excuse me, where's our room?" we asked the lad at reception, Danny looking fab in his Highland dress and me in my wedding dress (not a meringue, but definitely a wedding dress).

"Oh, er," he stuttered. "I'm sorry we're fully booked, there's a wedding on."

We looked at each other, the lad looked too embarrassed to be pulling our legs. My Mum had said she would book the room, perhaps she'd forgotten? Would we camp out on Uncle Henry and Aunt Anne's floor? Or with cousin Sophie, who had spent all evening with an open blouse and sloaney smile, checking for true Scotsmen, whilst her soon to be ex-boyfriend propped up the bar in his trousers?

"Oh! It's the bride and groom!" The young lad slapped his hand over his mouth, composed himself very quickly, then showed us to our four-poster bedroom. Sophie passed us on the stairs and had one last nationality check, on Danny. Bizarrely, I didn't mind – she's got lots of charm has cousin Sophie. And I'm sure Danny didn't mind either. Nice for a man to know his attractions don't stop the minute he gets married.

The Formula for Love

Apparently there's a formula for a man's perfect woman. Written by a man I'm sure, possibly even with sound statistical evidence to back it up. Who knows? Anyway, men want a woman half their age plus seven. So a 20 year old wants a 17 year old and a 40 year old, a 27 year old. This means, if you are going to live your life by a formula, that Danny and I were only right for each other for a fleeting moment, and that was years before we met. No wonder marriage can be such a struggle. And that's before you throw children into the equation. Amah was a year older than Ahcong, so the formula would never have fitted them, and they never exchanged a cross word in fifty nine years of marriage (to my knowledge, obviously). How did they manage that? Danny and I only managed to make it to the return drive from our honeymoon.

But there is no formula for love, just as there is no formula for life. And we're still here, nine years down the line, plus in-laws, dogs and children all requiring B and D love. Love can be exhausting! Now that I've got roots and offshoots and everything, what do I want? To have a bit less belonging and fly free? Oh that green, green grass of elsewhere!

* I've said enough about this in *Green Oranges on Lion Mountain*.

4. Am I Worth It?

Self-Esteem and the Respect of Others

"R.E.S.P.E.C.T." Arethra Franklin

"If you don't respect yourself, ain't nobody gonna give a good cahoot." The Staple Singers (1971)

"Our mission statement at Liveshy Nursery is to increase the self-esteem of every one of our children."

No, no. PLEASE don't increase Ella's self-esteem any more!

Out of 1.4 million species (and that's just the discovered ones), there are only one, possibly two, who have mastered fire and only two, possibly three, that show self-awareness. A psychologist called Lewis showed in 1990 that chimps could recognise themselves in a mirror, but baboons and gibbons couldn't. The mirror trick probably doesn't work under water so I don't think Dr. Lewis asked the dolphins, but they must be self-aware since they can talk (although mastering fire underwater is understandably tricky). Anyway, we humans take great pride, not only in how clever we are for being able to light a match, but also in our self-awareness. We're so complex! So sophisticated! Now we want to feel good about ourselves and for others to think we're marvellous too. Great. A whole extra rung of needs to fulfil.

Our 1,399,999 fellow species in the Kingdom of Life (plus, no doubt, the 30 million unnamed insects and bacteria) manage perfectly well without getting into a tizz about whether everybody loves them, or loves them enough, or respects them, or respects them enough. Life goes on, so they just get on with it. An antelope running away from a tiger has a safety problem, not an esteem problem. If the antelope wins the tiger's hunger needs are unfulfilled but he won't get upset about it. He'll just try someone slower.

R.E.S.P.E.C.T.

But have we really left all the rest of the animal kingdom behind on the safety rung (with perhaps a few higher mammals making it to the belonging rung)?

Well my mother would shout ANTHROPOMORHISM at me, but yes, other animals need respect. And not just chimps and dolphins. A tiger is pretty respectful of a spitting cobra (as indeed I would be), and then look at all that alpha male posturing and fighting in birds, frogs, elephants, and not to leave the girls out, there's the Queen Bee. And dogs. Dogs are big on respect.

The Dominant Dog

Would Dr. Maslow have anything to say about newly-weds wanting a puppy? Hmmm, don't know, but I'm sure Dr. Freud would have done. Nesting, probably.

Neither Danny nor I had ever had a dog, but we foolishly got two, arguing that dogs were pack animals. Rogie cried all night when we brought him home, a little puppy aged nine weeks deprived of the love of his mum and his litter, but soon cheered up the next day with the arrival of Bo.

From day one, team Rogie and Bo tried very hard to assert their dominance on team Danny and Em. "Woof, woof! Give us love!", they would bark, if shut out of the action. "Woof! You expect us to widdle on that newspaper? Woof! Don't crush our self-esteem!" (Okay, okay. Anthropomorphism, but without anthropomorphism we would never have had the pleasure of Baloo the Bear, and how much poorer would our lives have been?).

A psychiatrist friend of mine gave us a dog psychology book called *Why Does My Dog ...?* by John Fisher. The answer to why dogs bark/dig/chase cat was that 'dogs do.' According to Mr. Fisher, the bottom line with dogs is to master respect. The dog has to know you are the dominant dog, then it will respect you enough to sit, stand, heel, come etc., etc. If you let your dog assume Dominant Dog positions like sitting on the sofa, or in the doorway, or anywhere with a bit of height, then you are doomed. So you should make your dog watch you eat before you feed it, and never let it go into a room or through a gate in front of you.

Excellent advice of course, and if Danny and I had ever stopped fighting between ourselves over who was going to be dominant dog in our relationship, and applied some of Mr. Fisher's advice, we might have gained some control over our dogs (and subsequently our children) that would have made our lives immeasurably easier. Shit would still have happened, but in a specified place in the garden.

Anyway, my psychiatrist friend reckoned this dog psychology book was of much more use to him in his daily dealings with people than any other of the learned psychologists.

Self-Esteem

According to the majority of aforesaid learned psychologists, all our problems are due to a lack of self-esteem. Bullies, for instance, are just having a few esteem problems. Poor little Ghenghis Khan! You need to be loved and to belong, before you can have self-esteem. And you probably need to show that you can love and belong to earn respect. So how did the world's biggest bullies get to be so successful? Who gave them their feeling of self-worth? Well, most of them had a lot of love from at least one source (e.g.: Hitler's mother, Mrs. West, Mrs. Shipman, Mr. Thatcher). I'm not sure if there was a special someone who loved Ghenghis Khan, but perhaps Ghenghis was just born with so much natural self-esteem that he never gave a good cahoot about what anyone else thought.

In normal people it probably self-regulates. Too much self-esteem will lose you the love and respect that gave you your self-esteem in the first place; you lose your self-esteem and thus become a much nicer person, regaining some love and, hey presto, your self-esteem.

But it must be said that if you don't get love from the people you really want it from, then all the love in the world is not enough to make up for it, so you *still* don't have any self-esteem (e.g.: Princess Di).What a needy bunch we humans are! Frankly with all these variables, it's surprising we haven't all had nervous breakdowns.

Perhaps we shouldn't pay too much attention to what the psychologists say about self-esteem? After all, they have a vested interest in us all having nervous breakdowns. Maybe the great philosophers can do better?

As a group, the philosophers seemed well endowed on the self-esteem front, but often at the expense of the rest of their needs. Perhaps if you have enough self-esteem you don't need anything else? Socrates, for example, wandered around in dirty old robes and was entirely unbothered by the respect of others, suggesting we listen to reason rather than public opinion. But public opinion (excluding the views of Plato and a few other learned followers) didn't like to be so disregarded and Socrates was executed. The authorities forced him to drink a cup of hemlock. But Socrates had the self-esteem to stick by his beliefs to the bitter end (hemlock is indeed very bitter), thus gaining the respect of 2,000 years worth of public opinion. So we would probably call Socrates' self-esteem 'good'. (And I can therefore call my refusal to wear platform heels a philosophical statement against the unreasonable demands of public opinion, rather than the fear of falling off and twisting my ankle!). What about an example of less healthy self-esteem? Optimists shouldn't be bitchy, but no-one's perfect, so I think I'll choose a pessimist.

"It's bad today and every day it will get worse until the worst of all happens." Schopenhauer (1788-1860)

By all accounts (because obviously I've never met these people) Schopenhauer was not short of self-esteem, but clearly it didn't make him happy. He preferred the company of his poodles to other humans. Good or bad? Well, at least he recognised he needed some love from somewhere, if only a poodle.

Perhaps his poodles taught him some sense of responsibility for others, and in return Schopenhauer received total adoration from these beings who didn't care two hoots for his failings (that he never knew he had, attributing them to the failings of life itself)? Total, requited love from his dogs and thus self-esteem?

The Optimometer

To give Schopenhauer and all these other philosophical pessimists their due, it must be quite an achievement for a pessimist to maintain such self-esteem. Believing in yourself is generally an optimistic trait. My own esteem runs in direct proportion to my optimometer readings. Other variables are the tightness of my trousers, the amount of alcohol drunk (just enough boosts my optimometer readings, too much depresses them), stage of completion of tasks, or the behaviour of my children (delights or frights) and whether or not the person in the room with me is smiling, which will boost optimometer readings and esteem simultaneously.

If my optimometer readings are low, criticism will knock my esteem down much more than the equivalent compliment will boost it. Conversely, if my optimometer readings are riding high, I will interpret all potentially veiled criticisms as compliments.

"Your body's like a Volvo, Em. Sturdy and reliable." Dud the Stud, Unrequited Love No.6 *("In my defence I have never slept with more than one woman in 24 hours.")*.

Yes, but what young man wants a Volvo? Not even a self-confessed womanizer. By the end of the year, my relationship with Dud the Stud had progressed such that he called his camper van after me. Big, stubborn and slow? No, no, no. Perceive it as a compliment! (Easy, in retrospect.) Dud's camper van could travel the country, providing transport, shelter and accommodation. In Sierra Leone they told me: "Dr. Em you get body." Which meant:

"Dr. Em, you are fat." This was meant as a great compliment. To get body was to be healthy, and thus desirable, so I shall use that term from now on. "I get body" is so much more positive than "I am fat."

Now Draw a Moustache

Your children don't care if you get body or not (other than if getting body makes you go on a diet, thus making yourself irritable and liable to shout at them). They are much more straightforward.

"Have you got another baby in your bottom?" asked Art, when I was eight months pregnant. A bottom after all, is just at eye level for a child.

After a glass or two of wine, I can just about interpret this as a compliment: I had plenty of stores for times of famine for both me and my new baby.

"You look lovely, Mummy."

"Art! Why, thank you darling." This was better. Little boys were supposed to think their mothers beautiful. I smiled at my son, mascara pencil poised, and realised this was possibly the first time Art has ever seen me with make-up. I really should make the effort more often.

"Now draw on a moustache, Mummy."

Right. Interpret it as a compliment: who needs make-up, anyway?

The Iron Baby

Ella, aged two, appreciated my assets in their natural form.

"You've got nice brown eyes, Mummy."

"Why thank you darling."

"And I've got nice brown eyes, just like you."

And so she does, lovely brown eyes with eyelashes nearly as long as Art's, which can flutter and bat, and render all helpless in their wake. My little angel baby. Heartstoppingly beautiful, someone called her, with a smile that will inherit the earth and a soul of steel. My iron baby.

"Another story, Mummy." Flutter, flutter, great big smile.

"We've already had three stories. Well, okay. Last one."

Four stories. Five stories.

"One last story, Mummy?"

"No, that was the last one."

"One more story. Last one." She waved her forefinger at me.

"No, that's enough now darling. Night, night, Ella."

"Another story, mummy." Ella started sobbing. Tears pouring out of those nice brown eyes. "One more last one."

"No. Night, night, darling."

The tears stopped abruptly, and my three-year old little darling grabbed me by the lapels, pulling me towards her so that we glared nose to nose. "READ ME A STORY!"

And I'm sure there was just a glint of red in those nice brown eyes.

Okay, there's nothing attractive or healthy about false modesty and I should be pleased that my children are bursting with self-esteem. But the world (Western) has gone self-esteem mad. How much self-esteem do we need? Adverts suggest we can get it by buying a bigger, fancier car, or by buying a certain tipple and thus acquiring the most beautiful member of the opposite sex available to the casting agency for that shoot. Magazines tell you how to get more and more of it by self-improvement (body, financial, emotional, spiritual) or self-pampering and then there's the adverts inviting you to spend lots of money on yourself (and giving it to them) buying their shampoos, lotions and potions because "you're worth it".

But even Maslow suggested our self-esteem should be tempered by the respect of others, and who's going to respect a self-centred clever clogs? Certainly not a world full of other self-centred clever clogses. And surely it's not just the respect of others but respect *for* others too. So, yes, you might earn the respect of your friends by showing off that 20 carat diamond ring that your stunningly handsome fiancé bought you, but the ring on your finger may well have cost the hand of a woman in Sierra Leone.*

I can say I am worth it, as long as I remember to conjugate the full set:

I am worth it, you are worth it, he is worth it, she is worth it, we are worth it, you are worth it and they are worth it.

And what is 'it', if it's not shampoo? Whatever it is, it doesn't come in a packet.

* Unfortunately I'm not just being flippant here. Read *Blood Diamonds* by Greg Campbell and ask where your diamond came from.

5. Life Is A Lot Of Questions

Cognitive Needs

Philosophy. Philo = love. Sophia = wisdom

"Perfect humanity by cultivating the mind." Confuscius (551 – 479 B.C.)

"Je pense, donc je suis." Rene Descartes (1596-1650)

"Why do you have to anal–ise everything?" Nadine's Mum

Knowledge

My early self-esteem was founded on being a big enough clever fish at school, in the small pond that was Allanbank. I never mastered the Rubik's cube, nor read the classics, nor inherited my father's ability with crosswords, but I was good at passing exams with a minimum of effort. By the time I got to university, I was an intellectual minnow in the bigger pond of medical student smartarses. I left university for the big bad world, taking a bit of a departure via New Zealand and Sierra Leone, so you could say I became a toad, jumping around on the edge of the pond. My travels did at least expand the 'exploration' part of the cognitive rung, and probably did a lot more for my general knowledge and understanding of the world than any exam. Now, after three children (giving me new knowledge, like the names of Thomas the Tank engine's friends and new skills e.g.: how to assemble a Beyblade), I am the algae floating on the top. This is not meant to be self-deprecating. As I've mentioned, I'm a big fan of algae. They may be scum but, oh boy, did they earn their place in the ecosystem. Blue-green algae have been much more useful to the human race, and all of the animal kingdom, plus most of the plant kingdom, than the cleverest Nobel Prize winner. And that's without a brain between them.

Ernst Mair, an evolutionary biologist, argues that more stupid life forms are far better at survival than smart ones. Look at the cockroach! And what about Mike-the-Headless-Chicken* who ran around with no head for a year and a half? And the bacteria that live in boiling sulphur; you've got to be impressed with that. Not to mention the crafty old flu virus that mutates a little every season so we don't knock him out with our multi-million pound flu campaigns. Viruses don't have a brain either, or a body, or even a cell to call their own – they just borrow ours. Clever, eh?

But I don't want to underestimate the good old, grossly underused, human brain, Woody Allen's second favourite organ.

Steven Hawking's massive brain holds together a body that by anyone else's definition of his illness should long ago have ceased to exist. And Christopher Reeve gained more respect for his bravery in the face of his terrible personal tragedy than for pretending to be a Superman. Ten out of ten for Steven and Christopher for making the most of their potential.

But who really cares if it was the chicken or the egg first? Will that help get the dinner on the table? Possibly, if dinner's a choice between omelette or coq au vin.

The consolation of my intellectual decline has been watching my amazing children develop from helpless babies into cognitive beings, exploring and learning with endless energy and enthusiasm. I watch them and think, I used to be like that, I used to be excited by life and learning. But all is not lost - Ella has just turned three and slowly a little spark of interest is returning. Newspapers for instance. Not the proper news (too depressing for a recovering optimist) but little snippets – like the National Geographic pointing out that it must be the egg first. After all, dinosaurs were laying eggs long before chickens made an appearance. So the first ever chicken came from the egg of the Wild Red Jungle Fowl of India, and the first ever Wild Red Jungle Fowl came from the egg of a bird that wasn't quite a Wild Red Jungle Fowl and backwards in time to Mummy T-Rex's nice smooth pride and joy, nestled in her nest. Yes, apparently chickens are the closest living relatives of the T-Rex! And that little bit of knowledge gave me a frisson of satisfaction.

Understanding

So now my children sleep (most) nights and I don't have to pass any more exams, I can build on my new knowledge of little red hen's cousin T-Rex and start asking those pointless, esoteric questions. What is life?

"It's our perception of external reality which shapes our lives, not the reality itself." Carl Rogers, psychologist (1951)

In other words: life is all in your mind. So if it's in your mind, perhaps we better start asking questions.

Socrates asked questions all the time, probably really hard ones too, then (rather irritatingly) challenged all the answers. Aristotle came up with an answer to just about everything, from maths to astronomy to a moral structure for life, although some of those answers may have been wrong. Or maybe not. After all, we believed the world was flat, a logical enough conclusion from the information available at the time. Then Copernicus applied logic to new information and told us it was round, but perhaps there's another vital link that will disprove that too?

Exploration: The Man on The Moon

One of my favourite patients (let's call him Phil) never took the word of any scientist without challenging it. Nor did he believe their first cousin, the doctor, especially not their country cousin, the lowly GP. Phil was very poorly, but he defied death like he defied everything else, from his doctors to the ridiculous concept of man walking on the moon.

"Treatments are getting so much better, Phil. Even you must agree. And survival too. You never know what's out there: in the Amazon jungle, or from the space programme."

"There's bound to be something for me in the Amazon, if they don't chop it down before they find it, but not the space programme. What did NASA ever do?"

"Er. Land on the moon?" I suggested, a little surprised by the question.

"Don't tell me you still believe that we landed on the moon?"

"What? Well, yes, of course I do, I watched it! I was only six or something, but we all watched, cross-legged on the floor in the assembly hall."

"It was a hoax. A complete fabrication," laughed Phil.

"No ...?"

"Okay. Tell me why the flag was fluttering in the Apollo footage."

"Um ... It was windy?"

"Pah! How did you ever get through medical school? There's no atmosphere on the moon, so no wind."

"Oh. Right, of course. Maybe it was a downdraft?" I suggested, a little less sure of myself. "From the lunar module or something..."

"And how would a human ever survive the Van Allen Belt? That's over 300 rads of radiation circling the earth. You'd need a space suit that was four feet thick of lead ..."

"Really? Well, I don't ... What about your cough, Phil?" I was running about half an hour late now. "I'd better listen to your chest."

"And there were no stars," Phil persisted. "There's no clouds on the moon, so a perfect night sky. Why no stars?"

"Um, I don't know. Why on earth would they do it though? A great big hoax like that?"

"To distract the world from Vietnam, of course. And what about the actual film of all this so-called footage? How would it survive the extremes of temperature?"

"Wouldn't they have some sort of heat resistant containers?" We optimists tend not to be great believers in Conspiracy Theories.

"Heat resistant to 250 degrees?! Come on!"

"Okay, Phil, you've got me. Can I listen to your chest?"

Phil was back on chemotherapy when I went on maternity leave. All that unnatural crap he hated so much. We shook hands, surely for the last time. But no, there he was six months later, looking absolutely fine. For a few months. By the time I went on maternity leave again, he was terminal. We shook hands and said goodbye. He chastised me for the unseemly short gap between children.

A second bouncing boy later, with bags round my 'waist' and under my eyes, I returned to work and was surprised and delighted to see Phil's name at the end of my first morning surgery.

"Phil! I don't believe it!"

"It was the chemo making me poorly. Now I've stopped that poison and started eating some decent food, I'm fine. Have you tried the organic broccoli from Nature's Best in Fillstream?"

"Er, no. I usually do a supermarket sweep at Tescos."

"Shame on you! Watery, tasteless, exploitative veg from an evil multi-national that pumps water into its meat and squashes the little guy. And after you worked in Africa ..."

"Okay, I'll try harder. It's just the closest shop and easier with the kids... Anyway. I'm glad you're eating quality, but you need quantity too."

"I know. I'm still skinny."

"I'll donate you my spare tyre."

"No thanks. You're not the first to offer. I wouldn't mind a bit of buttock though, I'm getting pressure sores."

Phil's window of relative good health didn't last. He was back in hospital battling infection, hospital protocol and worse hospital food. Phil finally got home with a 24-hour carer, but cancer loves a man when he's down and soon he was really pretty poorly. Again.

"I'm putting my hopes on the eclipse. The eclipse in Leo, it's got to be significant! Not that I believe all that astrology nonsense either, but a bit of lunar therapy has to be better than all the crap you doctors keep feeding me."

I doubted he'd make it as far as the next new moon, never mind the eclipse, but although honesty was usually by far the best policy with Phil, this time I kept quiet. Phil didn't need me to point out how ill he was.

The eclipse came, and I went to visit Phil who was standing at the window (without a pinhole, of course).

"So doc, you were wrong again. I'm still here!"

"It looks like it."

"Next goal the Millennium?"

I smiled back wanly. The Millennium was really pushing it.

But if life can climb out of the primordial soup, then there's plenty of scope for miracles. A few strikes of lightening provided the primordial soup with its miracle and Phil reckoned that Boldham's partial eclipse gave him a partial cure.

"If I'd made it to Cornwall, I'd be cured now."

"Phil, you couldn't make it down the stairs, never mind Cornwall! But I'm impressed. Once again, you've proved us wrong. Last year, I would have given better odds for life on Mars than you making it this far."

"That's because there is life on Mars."

"Let me get this right. You don't believe that we walked on the moon, Phil, but you believe there's life on Mars?"

"Mars, or somewhere. Of course I don't believe we'll ever get through the Van Allen Belt to meet up, but yes, we're not alone. Why would we be?"

"Well, it was against so many odds that life even started once, never mind twice."

"All the elements of life are out there, floating around on bits of interstellar space dust. They've found amino acids and fatty acids on meteorites, you know."

"Fascinating. No, I didn't know that. How did they get past the Van Allen Belt to discover that, then?" I teased.

But Phil wasn't so easily beaten. "Radiation wouldn't affect an unmanned space probe, would it? Don't you know anything? What about the Green Bank Formula?"

"Er, Green Bank...?"

"It works out the number of stars being produced, and the fraction of those with planets, a goodly number which could sustain life**. The numbers are so huge. Miracles aren't rationed, you know. Don't you believe in miracles?"

"Well, it's a miracle that you're still here, Phil."

Phil's miracle lasted not just to the Millennium but for two years beyond. Then yet another cancer started, so quickly that his consultant admitted him directly to the hospice whilst he had radiotherapy. Coincidentally I was called to the hospice to sign a Part Two for a Cremation Form, and I took our medical student with me, to expose him to the administrative procedures associated with death. I was rather taken aback when we bumped into Phil in the corridor.

Phil was NOT pleased. He had always made it very clear that doctors were bad enough, but being paraded and prodded like a nameless 'case' in front of spotty, middle-class medical students was the pits. I didn't like to tell Phil that I was actually at the hospice to see a corpse, so I let him assume that I had indeed come to see him.

It wasn't just my middle-class student that had spoilt Phil's mood. The cancer was giving him horrible pain, and he felt we'd all been pretty slow in picking it up. I tried to explain that the consultant had sent him pretty promptly for a scan (well, in NHS terms) as soon as I'd referred him up with what was really only a funny little pimple, but there had been some delay on the reporting and it really was a dreadfully uncommon tumour in a dreadfully uncommon place.

"Well I've spent ten years getting f***ing uncommon cancers in f***ing uncommon places. And I'm sick of f***ing nurses coming in here wearing that same f***ing concerned look and asking me how I am today in that same f***ing concerned voice. And I tell them, f***ing awful, how the f*** do they think I feel? And then she asks me if I need to talk about it, well no I f***ing DON'T want to talk about it!"

Well, I am no psychiatrist, but this was the first time I'd personally seen Phil angry. It was clear that he did need to talk about it, but it was difficult to think of anything other than platitudes. Let's face it, Phil was right. He wasn't getting many of his needs met. No, perhaps he didn't want to talk about it, but he did need to talk about something.

"Er. I thought of you the other night. There was a programme on the faking of the moon landings." I was on dodgy territory here as I hadn't actually watched it.

"Yes, I saw it too," the student interjected. Bravo, spotty middle-class medical student! And even better, the student was an expert. "But if you read David Percy's book, *Dark Moon*, it's just full of inconsistencies."

"Says who? You?" Phil eyed the student, decided he was worth arguing with, and carried on. "Why no stars in any of the photos? I'll tell you. They didn't want the stars in because they couldn't work out what their configurations would be on the moon. And there are no stars in a studio."

"Stars are very difficult to photograph, you need a really long exposure."

"So why isn't there a crater under the lunar module, then? And why make the Apollo files classified until 2026?"

"Well..."

Phil died the following week, questioning everything until the end.

Socrates would have been proud of him, but I still believe man walked on the moon.

*Mike - the Headless Chicken.

Everyone knows a chicken can run around for some time without its head. In 1945 Mike lived for a year and a half. The farmer apparently aimed high with his axe as his mother-in-law was partial to 'a nice bit of neck'. Anyway, off came Mike's head, and Mike ran off. They waited a few minutes, and then a few hours, but he just kept going. So they started feeding him. Squirting food directly into his gullet was very successful as he gained weight from 2 1/2 pounds to nearly 8 lbs. He could feed (with help), he could grow, he excreted, he walked normally and apparently scratched for food – by all accounts, a happy, healthy chicken. I'm not sure if he reproduced (if anyone knows, do let me know), but his image was certainly reproduced extensively, on Time magazine and countless T shirts. So he lived against the odds, and is still famous, half a century later with a commemorative weekend each May in Fruita Colorado. Is that self -actualisation? It's certainly another ten out of ten for fulfilling potential.

**Green Bank Formula, Drake (1960's)

$N = R^*.fp.ne.fl.fi.fc.L$

Where R^* is the rate of star formation, fp the fraction of stars with planets, ne the average number of those planets that could theoretically sustain life, fl the fraction of these that actually go onto develop life, fi, the fraction of that life that develops intelligence, fc the fraction that forms civilisations x L, the expected lifespan of such a civilisation.

6. A Beautiful Life

Aesthetic Needs

life *laif, n,* ... the business and pleasures of the world

aesthetic *es-thet'ik, adj.* a sense of beauty ...the appreciation of beauty

"Pleasure is the beginning and the end of living happily."
Epicurus (I thought I'd just remind you of that one)

So now that we're fed, safe and sheltered, loved by ourselves and by others, we can start thinking about aesthetics: taking a leaf from Epicurus' garden and turning all your basic needs into pleasures. So dine rather than eat, take pleasure from the warmth of your fire in your beautifully decorated shelter, take pleasure from your discoveries (e.g.: that the chicken is the closest living relative of T-Rex) or from music or paintings or the natural world, or you can even take some moral high ground pleasure in the fact that justice has been done. Life is beautiful.

Outer Beauty

"One cannot make soup out of beauty." Estonian proverb

Just as I had problems with beautiful princesses who couldn't cope with peas under their mattresses, I struggled with ugly ducklings. Fantastic – the ugly duckling in question turned into a beautiful swan, good for him, but he was only accepted once he

71

was a beautiful swan. What if his feathers had stayed stubby and brown? Would it have been "Quack, quack, you're not worth it"?

The rare plain girl in a film only gets the guy after taking her glasses off and undergoing a massive makeover, then, gosh, look, it was Julia Roberts all along! That's all right then, she can have the guy. Conversely, the awkward, slightly nerdy guy often gets the most beautiful girl in the class after he's proved how kind, clever and fun he is. Great, I don't have a problem with his well-earned success, but kind, clever and fun nerdy girls don't get anyone. Not even the kind, clever and fun nerdy guy, because he wants the beautiful girl. It's not fair. But then, life isn't fair (and I suppose that realisation is the difference between optimism and delusion).

Health and Beauty

"Good health is the sister of beauty." Maltese proverb

Animals' attractiveness to the opposite sex is directly related to their health. They want a healthy mate for healthy offspring.

The slightly nerdy beta lion with a bit of a straggly mane and a limp is cast out of the pack to scavenge alone for eternity. Meanwhile, Mr. Muscles Shiny Mane gets all the women. Well I'm a nice, big, healthy specimen. Why did I have such trouble finding a mate? I hardly ever get ill, I have nice teeth, nice brown eyes just like Ella's, a nice smile and I do get body, which is a sign of good health in Sierra Leone (and thus beauty – yes!), so I reckon I would have done alright if I'd have been born a lioness. But I presume Maslow didn't mean 'are you personally beautiful?', rather that you have beauty in your world to appreciate. In which case I do very well. I've a nice view out the window, some pretty pictures on the wall and my children are particularly beautiful. No, they are. Really: Art's killer eyelashes, Frankie's dimples and Ella's nice brown eyes. Danny's not half bad either (except when he grows sideburns for some part in a play). And Rogie was gorgeous.

Rogie was just the most beautiful puppy you have ever seen. He managed to be sleek black, flouncy and fluffy all at once with a kiss curl atop his head, a white stripe down his muzzle, floppy white bib, and frilly white legs with big paws that he tripped over. We got him home that first day and lifted our wimpering nine week old pup from the carrier. But where was his tail? This doesn't say much for my powers of observation, but I suppose I had only been looking at his cuter end. Beauty surely doesn't involve losing a part of yourself? Suddenly I felt barbaric, not just for Rogie's docked tail, but for the whole concept of ownership over another species, impinging on their animal freedoms. Where was the justice in that? This was probably not the right time to start considering that whole argument, trying to rock, cuddle and console this poor motherless boy who was just crying pathetically – the poor pup that *I* had made motherless. Still, I couldn't stick the tail back on now, and he *was* gorgeous. We renamed him Rogie. The next day, puppy Bo arrived from the farm and Rogie Rogues cheered up enormously. The two puppy pals frolicked through the fields, a glimpse of spaniel ears flying above the golden buttercups ... Oh, they were beautiful.

"Beauty is in the Eye of the Beholder" (Greece, 300 B.C)

Not everyone likes dogs, just as everyone has a different concept of beauty. Breast implants/breast reductions, bottom implants/liposuction, nice big stately nose/pert button-nose job, perm your hair in the seventies/straighten it in the nineties, feed your girls up for marriage in Mali/starve them for the catwalk in Britain. And that's just visual beauty. The Booker judges notoriously disagree on the winner, there's beautiful and not so beautiful smells (we're probably much more in agreement with that, although my in-laws would spit out anything with the merest hint of garlic or spices, whereas I can't get enough), beautiful soft fur on an animal (not so beautiful off it) or a cosy bed/bed of nails. Then there's music. I had a patient complain (most vociferously) that playing classical music in the waiting room was making him ill and I, as a medical practitioner, should have been ashamed of myself for being so inconsiderate. It was soothing Beethoven, not discordant Schoenberg, possibly not to everyone's taste, but surely not offensive? The optimist's answer to differences in taste is to find beauty in everything.

"I never saw an ugly thing in my life." John Constable (1776-1837)

Order, Order

order *ör'dar, n.* ...a condition in which every part or unit is in its right place

entropy *en'tro-pi, n.* ...a measure of the disorder of a system. However, I prefer my Dad's definition: *"The tendency of the universe to chaos."*

There is beauty in order. If you ask a group of people to rank a series of people's photos in order of attractiveness, the more symmetrical faces come out top. Even babies seem to prefer the more symmetrical face, so are beauty and harmony all about order? Is life all about creating order from chaos? Trying to defeat entropy?

Order was never my strong point. I am much more of an entropy sort of girl. I can count and I am physically able to put things in order, it's just keeping them there that's the problem. Now I have children, the lack of order in our house is starting to get to me and I seem permanently stressed and grumpy at being unable to find keys, pencils, my glasses, my shoes, anything. Maslow is right to put order into our higher needs. We do need some order in our lives otherwise we end up paralysed by mess.

My mum started training to be a biology teacher when I was about eleven and decided to get a cleaner. I was horrified. "Other people's mums don't have servants! It's such a bourgeois thing to do." No wonder she didn't have any more children. Sorry, mum (but I remain unrepentant for hiding the cigarettes).

We had a great cleaner who helped us out in Boldham. Jessie came, created order from chaos (right down to combing out the rug fringes), then we came, felt briefly soothed by the beauty of order, and set to work creating chaos again. Entropy. What can I do? I'm just obeying the laws of the universe.

I'd been ranting and raving at Frankie about the enormous number of plastic toys strewn across the house, unappreciated, missing crucial pieces, stood on, discarded, totalling several months salary in Sierra Leone in original purchase cost. Shouting is not a fruitful activity as it makes me feel inadequate and stressed (and thus prone to shout more) and Frankie either ignores it, or bursts into tears. Instead I tried the careful explanation strategy so beloved of childcare manuals. I spent nearly an hour explaining famine, poverty, fair trade and cancellation of third world debt. I think he got it! That night, as I kissed him in his bed, Frankie said.

"Mum, I'm going to give my pocket money to charity."

"Well done, darling. That would be a lovely thing to do."

"Mummy?"

"Yes, darling."

"What's charity?"

"Well, it's when you give something to someone who doesn't have as much as you. Then you feel good."

"Okay, Mummy." Oh, what a wonderful parent I was! "Mummy?"

"Yes, darling?"

"If I give my pocket money to charity, can I have a Playstation?"

Inner Beauty

"I have been a selfish being all my life; in practice, though not in principle." Mr. Darcy, Jane Austen (1775-1817)

"I was going to save the world, but I couldn't find a babysitter." Colleen's fridge magnet

Justice

Are we any better? We may not be buying ourselves the possibility of a Playstation with our donation, but we usually want some recognition of our generosity in this life, or at least a place in heaven in the next. So charity is those with more, giving to those with less so they can feel virtuous about it, then continue to live with more, minus a tiny percentage, which is probably allowable against tax anyway. That's justice?

Giving to charity is intrinsically unjust, because why should you have more to give in the first place?

Life's not fair (as we have already firmly established). That's why. Where was the justice in the dinosaurs being wiped out by a dirty great big meteorite? What did the dinosaurs do to deserve that? Life may not be fair, but it does go on regardless. If you can't have dinosaurs, you can have chickens, or funny little mammals who somehow managed to survive a seven year winter, or if not funny little mammals, then you can have a cockroach. It seems you can always have cockroaches. Life is selfish; it will carve out a niche for itself that others vacate, or at the expense of others if they are not up to it. Survival of the fittest, not necessarily the morally superior. Do cockroaches fulfill any useful function in the great life cycle, for instance? One of the fittest perhaps, but are they worth it? What about my heroes, the blue-green algae? Mike-the-Headless-Chicken gets a whole commemorative weekend just for living without a head, and my algae don't even get a minute's silence. There's no justice there, either.

Having said all that, life has been more than fair to me, even though I have displayed most of the seven deadly sins and have singularly failed to display all of the eighteen virtues. If there was any justice in my world, or if indeed I wasn't just a fair weather optimist, I would be grateful instead of moaning all the time. Martin Seligiman, in his book *Authentic Happiness,* talks about learning to be grateful as a route to happiness. He's even got a gratitude questionnaire, the thought of which makes my British soul cringe, but there's a good point there. The Australians have a term: Whingeing Poms (I am Scottish and therefore excluded).

Mothers are always whingeing about how hard it is to juggle children and jobs, or about being bored stuck at home with children and no job; single girls are whingeing about not having a man, or a baby, or having to cover all the whingeing mums who do; our parents are whingeing about having to look after their parents, or our children; the employee moans about his boss; the boss about her employee; the landlord about her tenant, the tenant about her landlord; the doctor about her demanding patients, and the patient about his unsympathetic doctor. And everybody moans about not having enough money, even the rich (but not the VERY rich, who moan about having too much money which drives them to drink or drugs). And here I am moaning about people moaning. If we all stopped moaning, we could at least have the grace to take pleasure in our own good fortune and notice others to whom life has been much more unfair. That would be justice.

So perhaps we can redress the balance a bit by giving, but it probably only counts if you give something that you want, not that something for which you have no need, which is only cluttering up your space. Feel pleasure at decluttering and restoring a small corner of order? Fine. Feel pleasure that another person is making use of it rather than filling a landfill site? Certainly. Feel pleasure that some money has been made on the side for a worthy cause? No problem. But I don't think we can feel *virtuous* about getting rid of our unwanted cast-offs. Take the birthing chair.

The birthing chair was shipped over to Sierra Leone from an American donor at great cost. The fibre glass monstrosity resembled a big bath, suspended on a central mechanical pole that would electrically lift and lower the structure, with moulded leg-rests flung akimbo. This bloody thing sat in the middle of Serabu Hospital's delivery ward, getting in my way for two years because it was too heavy to move, terrifying the women, who never once, for the two years I was there, climbed into it to give birth. Because chances were, what with the electricity for only eight hours out of twenty-four, that if the power was on for them to get into it, it would be off by the time they needed to get out and they would be stranded. Then the rebels invaded Sierra

Leone. Serabu Hospital was burnt down in 1995. A friend sent me photos of the charred, roofless walls, being reclaimed by Mother Nature's green fronds. And there, in the midst of the remains of Serabu Hospital, stood the birthing chair, unscathed.

"There is nothing without purpose." Aristotle (384 -322 BC)

So, Mr. Aristotle, what is the answer to the great philosophical question of the purpose of that birthing chair? To show us there is no beauty in useless and expensive excess? Or to show that money not only cannot buy love, it cannot buy justice either?

How To Be Good

There it was, my first book, proudly displayed in the window of Waterstones the day after the launch. I dashed down the next day, clutching my camera, to record my auspicious rise to fame. But my book was gone. Instead the whole window was filled with *How To Be Good*. Hmmph. As if Nick Hornby needed any help! So I wrote to him, something like this:

Dear Mr. Hornby,

...you can imagine my dismay when I discovered I had been usurped by your tale of a female GP driven to distraction by her husband's new found moral zeal, while I a real-life female GP, am driven to distraction after two years in Africa, trying to sell enough books to help rebuild my hospital, burnt down in the civil war. So really the least you can do to reestablish your ethical credentials, is write me a foreward for my second edition ...

Well there's no foreward by Nick Hornby in *Green Oranges*, but in his defence he emailed an apology and sent me a donation for my hospital by return post. After that, I thought I really better read *How To Be Good* which, though I hate to say it, was really very good, although it didn't really answer the question.

Never mind; the Oxford Dictionary to the rescue:

good *good, adj.* having the right or desired qualities

What qualities are those then? Over to that clever chap, Aristotle.

Balance

Aristotle had a great long list of desired qualities, but, even without a wife or children, he rather wonderfully decided that too much virtue was also a vice. He said it was all about balance. For example:

Vice of Deficiency	Virtuous Mean	Vice of Excess
Cowardice	Courage	Rashness
Surly	Friendly	Obsequious
Shamelessness	Modesty	Bashfulness
Boorishness	Wittiness	Buffoonery
Do nothing	Do good	Holier than thou

The last one is mine (inspired by Mr. Hornby's book).

Anyway, you get the picture. My dad has a similar philosophy (although usually applied to food and drink rather than virtue): Excess in Moderation. Although I think Aristotle was possibly aiming for Moderation in Excess. Anyway, I like the idea that it's actually sinful to be too good, which will allow me to enjoy the pleasures of the world. The sin is to fail to be grateful for my great (undeserved) good fortune. After all, it gives me a warm glow to see my children enjoying themselves, so I wouldn't want God to be deprived of that parental warm glow toward his human race. Gosh, I've managed to argue myself out of giving anything up at all!

I'm not sure God would agree. Ah. God. Now there's an expert I haven't really consulted.

Truth

Is there a God?

Oh dear, another big question, and I haven't come up with a decent answer to the meaning of life yet. Maybe "Is there a God?" should have been the first question? Maybe I'm just too scared to ask? If the answer is *yes*, am I going to have to give up chocolate, alcohol and my nice house to prove it? Equally, there would be something very depressing about finding the answer is *no*. Of course, I would only want the answer to be *yes* if God was the sort of God I wanted, ie: not the sort of God who sends floods and swarms of locusts, then has his angels fold their arms/wings, sniff disapprovingly and tell me I just wasn't good enough to pass through the Pearly Gates because I never *could* bring myself to give up chocolate.

I want to believe in a God who is kind and generous and responsible for everything and has a great plan and will look after us all for eternity, even if there are a few hiccoughs in the brief time we inhabit our human bodies. I really, really want to believe that I won't really die, and my children and loved ones will never die either, but we will stay in heaven for ever and ever and finally understand. My God would be a communal sort of divine being, who's not too fussed about where we live or what culture we were brought up in, or what stories we were told about Him/Her as a child. He/She probably doesn't mind if we give our religions names and rules and stories as He/She knows the whole *meaning of life/is there a God* questions are just too difficult for us to understand, so we need some sort of a framework to get started on. And, of course, we humans love to show off our unique talent for communication with stories and metaphors, all with our own local twists.*

But whether you're Jewish, Hindu, Buddhist, Taoist, Christian, Islamic, Zoroastrian, Vegetarian, Humanist, Agnostic, Atheist, Plain Confused or Always Questioning (a la Socrates and Phil), we all have a version of '*do unto others as you would have done unto yourself*'. In Sierra Leone it's: *You du me, I du you*. Once 'you do me and I do you,' then after that, truth is being true to yourself. That's how to be good.

* Here's how I understand religious 'differences', after a quick look in *Religion FOR DUMMIES*.

Judaism, Christianity and Islam. (in order of appearance) There is only one God, who gave us free will to decide how we would live and some commandments as a moral code.

Judaism. According to the Hebrew Bible, their Messiah will bring world peace and a gathering of Jewish exiles, which Jesus didn't do. They don't believe their God would ever become human and the Christian Trinity sounds a bit like three Gods rather than one. Life is a gift from God that he can also take away.

Christianity. One God, but with a personal Messiah by the name of Jesus, giving a Trinity of God the Father, God the Son and God the Holy Spirit. They incorporate the Hebrew Bible as the Old Testament, and have added a sequel, the New Testament, to form the Christian Bible.

Islam. There is no god but God, and Mohammed is his prophet. Jesus was a great prophet too, but was unable to complete his mission, so more guidance was needed in the Qur'an, which could be viewed as a sequel to the Christian Bible. The Qur'an is the perfect transcription of the infallible word of God, so should be read, or heard, in Arabic, rather than end up with the chinese whispers effect of translation which causes so much theological argument between Christian Sects.

Taoism. Founded by Lao-Tzu, a philosopher 2,000 years ago. Simplicity and selflessness, in conforming with the Tao (the Way). Everything moves from non-being to being to non-being. Allow the Tao to flow unchallenged and the world becomes a tranquil place.

Hinduism. Lots of gods and goddesses but one divine essence, the Braham – an eternal, infinite principal with no beginning and no end, the source and substance of all existence. They believe in reincarnation and Karma, where things you do in this life have a bearing on what you will be in your next life. If Brahman is the creator God, they have a destroyer God, Shiva, and a destroyer Goddess, Kali.

Buddhism. Nothing lasts. Suffering comes from being attached to the things of ordinary existence.

7. The Dizzy Heights

Self-Actualisation!
(Becoming all you are capable of becoming)

"We can't all do everything." Virgil (70-19 B.C.)

"Climb every mountain... follow your dream." Maria Von Trapp

According to Maslow, only two percent of us ever achieve self-actualisation, so how are you ever going to make it to the top rung? Or should you make it there at all, when really the self-actualisers are so few, and it's really rather a selfish thing, isn't it? Self-actualisation. It's something that we can never get enough of. Usually, once you have had enough air to breathe, you don't go looking for more, ditto with sleep and water (although my argument falls down with certain people who are always looking for food and sex). But once we achieve our personal goals, we just keep setting more and harder goals for ourselves so that we never glory in reaching the pinnacle. Or perhaps we only reach the pinnacle by sacrificing a basic need, like food to be a supermodel, or food, sleep and warmth to climb Everest (or your poor family left at home), or sleep to pass your exams. It might get you a brief visit to the top (very brief in the case of the Everest climber), but it won't keep you there. Life will throw some disaster or disappointment in your way to knock you off your perch, you can bet on it. This might not be my most optimistic statement, but even optimists need to be realists.

If we can't reach a permanent place at the top of the pyramid, we might manage one of Maslow's *Peak Experiences*. A Peak Experience loses you in the moment of your own achievement such that nothing else matters: the Olympic gold medallist crossing the line, orgasm, a bullfighter killing the bull, childbirth, walking on the moon, somebody telling you they liked your book. The trouble with peak experiences, apart from being intrinsically selfish, and not always 'good', is that they only leave one way to go. Down.

What human achievement could be more self-actualising than walking on the moon, for instance? Then what? The astronauts all did quite badly by all accounts, suffering mental illness and early deaths. I would say that's the trouble with too much achievement; all you want is more, more, more. (Phil, of course had a different explanation for the astronauts' psychological problems: they couldn't live with the knowledge of their great deceit).

Tips For The Top

Dr. Maslow suggested that a self-actualised person should possess the following qualities: spontaneity; creativity; a philosophical sense of humour; a sense of playfulness; the ability to forge profound personal relationships; empathy to the needs of others; a democratic character structure; a need for privacy; and a resistance to allowing their sense of what is right to be overturned by the whims of fashion or other cultural influence. And, of course, they have already fulfilled all the needs on the lower rungs. Gosh! The pressure's on. Let me see if I fulfil any of the criteria to join Dr. Maslow's exclusive club. I may need to apply a bit of creative optimism to this one...

Spontaneity

If we substitute the word 'disorganised' with 'spontaneous', then I get a big tick.

Profound Interpersonal Relationships

Well, I've got some good pals, my cousins, aunts and uncles and parents are all good fun and there's Danny and the kids.

Democratic Character Structure

Too damn democratic sometimes - seeing every side of an argument can be so exhausting. I think a bit of straight dictatorship would do all my family a big favour.

Creativity

I think I do quite well on this one. I may not be very good at baking cakes, but I've got good ideas for decorating them – from a scaled representation of my grandparent's house, Monikie, for their wedding anniversary, Rogie and Bo shaped cakes and a crossword puzzle for my Dad with sugar letters so he could fill it in.

Unfortunately creativity is on the top rung and I'll never get past the 'order' bit on the aesthetic rung below to qualify. Perhaps you can't be endowed with both creativity and order, or is that just my excuse for being a domestic slob? Oh, and I've had three kids. That must count as creativity?

Philosophical Sense of Humour

Hmmm.....
Why did the chicken cross the road?
Socrates – is there any logical reason why he shouldn't?
Seneca – he was doomed anyway.
Epicurus – for pleasure.
Nietzsche – for pain.
Neil Armstrong – one small step for a chicken.
Phil – he never crossed the road!

Maslow – one small step to self-actualisation ...
Descartes – he crosses the road, therefore he is.
The egg – he just wanted to be first.
T-Rex – Hmmph! Evolution's just gone too far.

A Sense of Playfulness

"Life is for having fun!" Art (7)

Oh, well done Dr. Maslow for including pleasure's childish sibling, fun. Mind you, the great minds are all waking up to the importance of fun. Now you can get courses and workshops on laughter and humour, such as that American philosopher I mentioned before, John Morreal, with his *Philosophy of Laughter*. Of course, once you start studying humour, it ceases to be fun. Children manage to laugh over 150 times a day without having to study it, whereas we clever adults average a paltry 17. Fun should be on every rung without having to think about it. Fulfil your basic needs, then have fun. No. Have fun fulfilling your basic needs and you're half way to self-actualisation! And how do I do? Well, I just seem to be too tired to have fun these days. Must do better.

The Need for Privacy

Is Danny reading in the toilet just trying to self-actualise?

As an only child, I hated privacy, now I lock myself in the bath so the children can't get in.

But privacy is a cultural need. "I want to be alone" wouldn't gain you any respect in Sierra Leone.

Resistance to Cultural Influences

Was I self-actualised by not wearing platform shoes? Are the Westerners wearing short shorts in Africa being self-actualised or just plain rude?

Empathy

I thought I was a pretty empathetic person and used to be a little irritated/insulted when people said "you don't understand, you haven't suffered x, y, z.". One particular bugbear phrase was, "you don't understand, you're not a mother."

Well, they were right, I didn't.

Gravida One - An Enormous Pork Pie

I didn't particularly want children in my teens or my twenties. It all seemed rather boring. My friends who were lumbered with children all became rather boring too, as I have become – you just don't have the energy to be fascinating company, and you can never finish a conversation without some disaster befalling a piece of crockery, or a plant or another child, or, your own child at the hands of someone else's child, or indeed, at the hands of another of your own children. But the old biological clock ticks on and you start wanting a baby. Not necessarily 'wanting children'. Everything is geared towards the pregnancy, childbirth and having a baby. There's remarkably little about quite what you're going to do with it when your little bundle of noise actually arrives, which is why we're all so unprepared.

But I was lucky and pregnancy wasn't really much of a problem. When you start out at 11 stones, then adding a bit of baby here and there didn't make that much difference. My morning sickness was blessedly minimal, with only one vomit. Unfortunately that one vomit was in a patient's garden, which I tried to bury under the pansies (driving round Boldham at rush hour is a nauseating experience at best). Then Ahcong broke his hip, which distracted me from baby thoughts. (We made the 15 hour round trip to Strathfarrell as often as we could and showed Ahcong the twenty-week scan photos of his first great-grandchild. My grandfather was failing fast, but he had understood.) Sadly, he died soon after - the end of an era and devastating for Amah. But he'd had such a good, happy life, that really, what more could you ask for? Maslow gave some twenty or so examples of the self-actualised person, including the likes of Abraham Lincoln, Eleanor Roosevelt and Albert Einstein. What? Only twenty? In the whole history of the human race? But of course Dr. Maslow never actually met Ahcong, my Grandad.

I don't think I really believed that I, of all people, was actually going to have a baby. My friends couldn't believe it either. Sam's partner, Anton, decided that I was probably going to surprise us all by giving birth to an enormous pork pie. I stayed at work until I was eight months pregnant, harbouring under the romantic illusion that the longer I worked the more time I would have with my adorable little baby when she came.

I was blooming. I was healthy. I had all my basic needs met: we had a nice, safe house; I had love; I belonged; I was a partner at West Hill Surgery, a cosy two partner GP practice in a lovely city and from time-to-time I even did a bit of good for my patients; I was writing a book about Sierra Leone and I had accepted my body, which for all its faults, was clearly functional and pregnant people weren't expected to be skinny. And I was heading for one of Maslow's peak experiences. Childbirth.

Childbirth - A Peak Experience?

A Chicken Madras with Sam and Anton was enough to leave me standing in a pool of amniotic fluid at midnight in the kitchen, three weeks early. Bo didn't like it at all. She cowered under the kitchen table, flattened her big floppy spaniel ears against her head and whimpered. Amniotic fluid must have some primeval animal smell, warning others to avoid a bitch having pups. Rogie, however, was quite excited by it all. We had to stop him licking it off the floor. Must just be a girl thing. Or perhaps it's just that Rogie, great beauty that he was, remained just a few licks short of a lollipop?

Di, the midwife, was quite happy for me to stay at home until I started 'proper' contractions.

"You mean these pains aren't 'proper' contractions?"

Apparently not. As a doctor who'd seen all manner of obstetric problems in my two years in Africa, I assumed I knew all about it. Yes women seemed to find it a bit painful, but it couldn't really be that bad, surely? Not for a straightforward delivery.

"You'll have to go in, whether you're contracting or not, at midnight tomorrow. That'll be twenty-four hours after your waters have gone."

"Or I'll turn into a pumpkin? I was rather hoping I'd lose the pumpkin. I'm not sure I fancy twenty-four hours of this."

"Why don't you have a nice hot bath?"

By morning, my contractions were still irregular, so I thought I'd try a walk with Danny. Bo refused to leave her basket. "Okay, Bo Bo, I'm having a baby. So what? Like it or lump it. Walkies?"

Bo curled herself into a tighter ball, and buried her nose in her paws.

Rogie at least enjoyed the walk, but the brisk activity and gravity failed to bring on 'better' contractions, so I tried washing the car instead (the only other time I ever washed the car was the day before we sold it). That did the trick, things were getting really rather painful. So when Di popped in on her way home, I expected her to gasp with amazement at my bravery and send me straight in, to deliver my first born, seconds after arriving. Or perhaps I'd even left it so late that Danny would have to deliver me dramatically in the back seat of the car.

"You're not in labour yet," announced Di.

"What do you mean, not in labour? You haven't even examined me."

"I can tell you're not in labour, you're not distressed enough."

Thanks a lot, pal. And I used to think Di was a great midwife. "But I'm just being brave!"

"Okay, then, let's have a look." Di examined me. 2-3cm dilated. Not in established labour. Hmmph. "Why don't you take a bath?"

So I took another hot bath, then reapplied the sticky pads of the dodgy TENs machine I'd borrowed from the practice (or rather bought especially for the practice as I felt we really ought to have one to lend out and I, coincidentally, would be the first borrower). Anyway, despite being wired up to the little box of electric shocks, the bloody thing cut out every time I hit the boost button. If I turned it down, then slowly back up again I could bypass the problem, so it certainly worked as a distraction tool, although I would argue about its analgesic properties.

So far the 'Peak Experience' wasn't impressing me. Considerable pain and no food all day.

When I could bear it no longer, I got out of the bath and Danny drove me into the hospital. It was only 20 minutes in the car at nine o'clock at night, but it seemed an eternity. I felt sick, I couldn't get comfortable, I felt sick, it was too painful, I felt sick, really sick, I was going to be sick. I motioned frantically to Danny, who could see me gagging and screeched to a halt. I was sick. All over a passing pair of bare legs in white Jimmy Choos, on their way to a night out in Boldham. Okay, I doubt they were Jimmy Choos in Boldham, but I didn't hang about to ask.

"Sorry," I muttered contritely.

All I can say about the rest of it was that I wish I'd been nicer to all those women I'd had to look after in labour as a junior doctor on the delivery suite and then in Sierra Leone. I'd written one of those pretty pointless birth plans, stating in black and white that I wanted a natural birth, so no epidurals. What pointless bravado! I WANTED AN EPIDURAL! The hospital midwife read my birthing plan and suggested a bath.

"What about painkillers? Morphine?," I begged. "An epidural?"

"After the bath."

Finally she gave me a syringe full of pethidine. It just made me sick. I won't bore you with the next four hours, but eventually I was in second stage. I'd been full of bright ideas of squatting, or other much more physiological positions, but by this time my legs were total porridge and I couldn't move up the bed. I didn't want to push either; it was too bloody sore. I looked at the clock. "Oh God, I'm a primigravida and that means I'll be at this for at least an hour, and that's if there's no problems. I don't think I'll last an hour. Sorry, sorry to all those labouring women in my care that I wasn't nicer to."

Perhaps I was forgiven, for 20 minutes later, I landed my first baby like a fish. Wow! Peak Experience! Arthur Pike, after Ahcong, his Great Granddad. Life's a bloody miracle. That's what it is.

Section 2

Tumbling Off The Pyramid

8. Back to Basics.

"Try to come to terms with your wishes and reality. We are made angry by dangerously optimistic notions of what the world is like." Seneca (4 B.C. – 65 A.D.)

"Expectation management." Danny

Breast is a Beast, sorry, Best

There's nothing like having a baby to knock you right off your pyramid. Forget self-actualisation, forget truth and justice, forget beauty, forget knowledge and exploration, forget self-esteem, forget sleep. Someone else's needs suddenly become your whole responsibility.

For every peak experience there's a trough, and for me the peak experience of childbirth was rapidly followed by the trough of failure. I was struggling to provide Art's most basic need. Food. I couldn't breastfeed.

Helen's Nipples

As a pregnant woman, lovingly rubbing the swell of my belly, I assumed I would be a laid-back sort of mother who would nurse her baby effortlessly. After all, I've coped with cardiac arrests, surgery with a book of instructions in one hand and a kerosene lamp in the other, rebel invasions, disobedient dogs and drug addicts. How hard can suckling one tiny baby be? Ha!

"Perfectly natural, why all the fuss?" I would think, just stopping short of voicing my disapproval at the majority of my patients who were thrusting plastic teats in their tiny babies' mouths by the time they came to see me for their six-week check. Women have been breastfeeding worldwide, along with the rest of the mammalian kingdom, back to before the dinosaurs. Dinosaurs of course didn't have to worry about breastfeeding (no wonder they survived 150 million years!) So what was my problem?

Big boobs. Women always worry that their breasts aren't big enough to breastfeed, but it's the big-breasted women who have the problem. It's like trying to suck on a basketball...aaah....aaahh.... no way your little baby can get his mouth round them, especially when you've got flat nipples and your breasts are engorged with milk. A nice dangly udder is a much better arrangement, or even just nice, pert breasts with big, sticky-out nipples. My friend Helen had the most extraordinary nipples. They were so prominent that they had worn a hole through her squash bra, one juicy nipple poking out on each side. How I laughed! Helen, of course, had no trouble breastfeeding her children, just as she had no trouble thrashing me at squash. I take it all back Helen, my pyramid for your nipples!

Failing at anything doesn't do much for your esteem, and then there's the loss of self-esteem that goes with lying in a hospital bed. I'd never seen a hospital ward from the patient's bed before and suddenly I understood what Phil had been complaining about all those years of his illness. What a palaver. Can't count how many people came in to mop the floor, change the water in my jug, check I was taking my pills (iron tablets that I was carefully not taking till my tail end healed up as iron can make you constipated, and with the state of my nether regions, constipation was something I could do without), give out the baby bounty bag, take the newborn baby photos and then there were the visits from various midwives and students and the consultant ward round (at 1.30pm, ie: slap in the middle of quiet hour, the only chance to get a nap). And of course the breastfeeding counsellor who said 'breast is best' six different times in six different ways, then gave me a handful of leaflets with babies at the breast smiling gratefully up at their mothers. Talk about managing expectations! My baby was screaming and wouldn't start smiling for six weeks (if, indeed, he ever did, right then it didn't seem very likely) - these angelic babies in the photo were at least four months old.

"Look, it's not that I don't know about all the benefits of breastfeeding, but I can't get him to latch on."

"Keep trying. Breast is best," chirped the breastfeeding counsellor and then she left. If I'd have had my wits about me, I'd have pinned her down at the door and forced her to give me some practical help on how to do it, not rub my nose in my obvious inadequacy. Instead, I just burst into tears. And that's me as a doctor, who has some experience, and loads of theoretical knowledge of what it ought to be like. God help the rest of the new mums. It's no wonder breastfeeding is at such pathetically low levels. I foolishly stayed in hospital for four days, much longer than I might otherwise have done. This was my attempt to be 'sensible' for a change and stay where help was on hand until I could get Art to suck. Trouble was 'help' all had a slightly different opinion. Thou shalt never use a nipple shield. Have you tried a nipple shield?

After four days of screaming baby (poor little critter was hungry), screaming mum, tattered nipples, Daisy the electric pump etc. etc., it was obvious Art was never going to latch on. I was finally persuaded to put on the silicone sombrero, peppered with holes, lining up boob, nipple shield and baby, then open wide and plug in. And Art plugged in. He was glued on, and sucked and sucked and sucked. After about half an hour, he just fell off, his face purple with the effort, the circular imprint of the nipple shield round his mouth and excess milk dribbling from the side of his mouth. Total satiation. Total satisfaction. Thank God!

The next feed, I produced my nipple shield from the little pot of sterilisation fluid, plumped up my pillows and applied my fake plastic nipple when the next midwife appeared.

"Oh you really mustn't use a nipple shield, it reduces the milk flow."

"But I can't get him latched on."

"You've got to keep trying, breast is best. Pip pip."

Aaaagh!

Think Cow

Things never really improved when I got home. A friend told me the best advice she had was to sit back and 'think cow'. Clearly, I needed to relax. Five nights without sleep was sending me a bit psychotic (as already shown by scientific and Nazi experimentation). Di said (very gently) that I really shouldn't use a nipple shield as it reduced the milk flow and detracted from the full, natural, audiovisual, olfactory, tactile, pseudo-sexual, bonding, hormonal, ecstatic, religious, interactive experience that is breastfeeding. She suggested using the breast pump to make a proper teat shape before even trying, but Art was having none of it. I spotted a Nazi torture chamber device on the bottom shelf at Tescos, which you clipped on to the nipple and left on all day. It said on the packet that if you wore it every day for months then you'd get nipples that would put Helen to shame, without resorting to plastic surgery. It actually said that on the leaflet, not the bit about Helen's nipples of course, the bit about plastic surgery. Really? Women would actually do that? Anyway, Art still couldn't get a grip. The nipple shield at least got him fed. Vikki, another midwife, gave me a book called, yes, you've guessed it, *Breast is Best*.*

Breast is Best could be summed up in three words: thou shalt breastfeed. There was one line in it that particularly got me. It went something like this: if you're at your wit's end and ask someone what to do, and they advise you to give up, then ask someone else. Of course there was no way that *Breast is Best* advised using a nipple shield and if indeed you had succumbed on the advice of some philistine that didn't know any better, then you needed to get your baby off ASAP. They suggested gradually snipping away at the tip until there was nothing left, like my baby teeth when they finally came out, worn down by teeth grinding, leaving only the rim left, like a sucked down polo. A GP friend of my mum's hypnotised me to stop grinding my teeth when I was ten. Worked perfectly after only two sessions, which just goes to show the power of the old mind over matter thing.

Hmm, perhaps Art and I should have tried hypnosis, to relax us into the perfect breastfeeding pair? Think cow.

Strictly Breastfeeding

Breastfeeding is just like ballroom dancing, you see. You just need practice, and preferably with a partner who knows what he is doing. And some are born naturals and some are not. Obviously I just have two left boobs. Of course in other countries they accept that a first born baby and first born mother is as bad as throwing two virgins together on their wedding night and are very practical about it. Give the new mum someone else's experienced baby and give the baby an experienced mum, then once both sides have got the idea, swap back. (And I think they have a similar solution to the virgin problem too). A new reality TV show: *Strictly Breastfeeding*?

Naturally our sensitive Western sensibilities would consider this disgusting. We in the West seem to think sobbing uncontrollably, alone at four o'clock in the morning, trying to read *Breast is Best* through your tears, with a baby plugged into his plastic sombrero for hours on end is a preferable, more tasteful option. So no sleep, no self-esteem, and there wasn't a lot of bonding going on, either.

Bring me Sunshine

Breastfeeding badly all night is one of the most depressing, lonely experiences I have had. Friends told me that it wouldn't last forever and it would get better in time, but how long? Years later? Months later? Weeks later? Days later? Even hours later was too long for me at two in the morning. What had happened to the optimist? Perhaps you can only be an optimist whilst you're climbing Maslow's pyramid, then become a pessimist on the way down? Sometimes I put on the radio, or a talking book, as even the telly had shut down, apart from Open University, although I did watch the full, unabridged Oscars and the full General Election results.

Somehow breastfeeding badly at 8am after no significant sleep didn't seem so bad. It must be something to do with the prospect of daylight through the window, stimulating your pineal gland and boosting your melatonin levels. Melatonin helps jet lag, insomnia, increases lifespan and improves your sexual drive – if you believe the internet adverts.

You can get light boxes for people with SAD (Seasonal Affective Disorder), which seems to help their symptoms of depression, and for shift workers, to counter their bodies' totally unreasonable desire to be asleep in the dark of night. Those residents of Nordic countries use them regularly to get them through the winter. Maybe this is the answer for the world's newborn mums? Sit in front of a light box pretending you are basking in the Caribbean sun. I suspect the light box wouldn't work so well as actually basking in the Caribbean. (Did I mention light as a basic need? Sorry, can't remember. My brain has shrunk through pregnancy and childbirth, or perhaps it's just going on strike until I do something about getting my sleep deficit out of the red?). Maybe this is why African mums seem to manage breast feeding absolutely fine. Lots of sunlight to stimulate their pineals, so even if they don't actually get any more sleep, at least they feel better about it. Or perhaps I'm just a wuss?

Danny finally confiscated *Breast is a Beast*, whoops, sorry, *Breast is Best*. It now lies at the bottom of some Yorkshire landfill site, communing with nature at the most basic level, shouting abuse at all the disposable nappies that keep landing on top of it. And no I didn't wash my own nappies. Too bloody knackered and too bloody lazy, who knows? I wasn't caring too much for the environment, or anything else, anymore.

All this tending to other's needs makes you neglect your own needs. My undercarriage was rather shambolic and needed attention. In my capacity as doctor, the Senior Registrar sewed up my second degree perineal tear, rather than the duty midwife. The senior doctor made a beautiful job, or so she told me, with neat, unseen, sub-cuticular sutures that wouldn't need removing. It all fell apart at day six. Di said she couldn't remove those fancy stitches as they were sort of buried. By the next day, they weren't buried at all. I could feel them, forming a little ladder of stitches all down my perineum. With a bit of imagination, I could just about use them to strum out *House of the Rising Sun*.

In Africa I had learnt (the hard way) that there was no point trying to hold a collapsed wound together. You just needed to open it up to heal naturally. Di agreed and snipped a few rungs, but this wasn't enough to breach the barrier of the Senior Registrar's perfect stitching. That night, I lay in the bath, half asleep, idly twanging my stitches. No, they had to go! I took a pair of nail scissors and (look no mirrors!) snipped each rung, until the whole thing fell apart. Ah. Bliss! I then spent a happy half hour pulling out all the shreds of thread that remained. Until Art stopped my fun, screaming for another feed.

Well, my tail-end healed eventually, as everything pretty well does, no matter what you do. The body is truly a remarkable thing. In fact, there are a number of studies (that if I get keen I may even quote and reference for you at the end, but then again both you dear reader, and I, may get too tired to bother) that have shown you can get just as good a result by not sewing up the smaller tears at all. Just leave them open in the first place, to heal from the bottom up. Gets a neater, less infected end result in the long run, with much less pain and subsequent problems, but we in the West don't like it as it's untidy (just as we don't like swapping babies for breastfeeding practice). Gosh, we do make life difficult for ourselves sometimes.

Looking back, I wonder why I did find it so hard. Danny, with his IT Consultant hat on, says it's all to do with expectation management. You've got to lower your expectations, right down to the bottom rung. Expecting, wanting, my higher needs to be fulfilled (ie: to carry on having a life like before), or even expecting my all my basic rung needs (like sleep) would be fulfilled. Art needed milk, and that was it, really. That should have been my only expectation. Forget self-actualisation, forget truth and justice, forget beauty, forget knowledge and exploration, forget self-esteem, forget sleep. Think cow.

Breastfeeding References

If you type Breastfeeding into the search engine of the online book retailer, Amazon, you get 384 entries! These are the ones I've read:

Breast is Best by Dr. Penny Stanway. Actually full of useful info, if rather religious! I believe it has been updated and reissued in 2005.

So That's What They're For by Janet Tramaro. Rather American, but lots of useful and fascinating info. She tries to hide her religious fervour behind amusing anecdotes.

What To Expect When You're Breastfeeding by Clare Byam-Cook. Advocates not beating yourself up and even advocates having a life! She's also made a practical video: *Breastfeeding Without Tears*.

There's lots of useful info and support on www.breastfeeding.co.uk, but it can be a bit guilt inducing if you do decide to give up.

And see chapters 15 and 16!

9. Life Begins at Home

*"Life is adapting to change. Which is why I married you,
the most adaptable person I have ever met - until you had
children."* Danny.

"Reasons To Be Cheerful. Part 3." Ian Dury.

Bottle- feeders Anonymous

Alcoholics never recover, and neither does a mum who gives
up breastfeeding. I still feel guilty to this day (hence the whole
preceding chapter protesting too much). People talk about being
embarrassed to breastfeed in public, but I was embarrassed to
bottle-feed. A paediatrician friend of mine had similar problems
and we thought we should start a new group, Bottle-feeders
Anonymous.

In Search of My Lost Esteem

It wasn't just the breastfeeding that was upsetting Art, it was
being landed with me for a mother. Breastfeeding is supposed to
be the greatest bonding experience for a mother and babe, but
when the baby can't do it, and he's hungry, perhaps he panics
and loses confidence? If he thinks his hunger needs won't be met,
he doesn't totally trust that his mother will meet his other needs.
And his mother doesn't totally trust herself either.

There are those who are natural mothers and there are
those who are not. I was not, and I really didn't like feeling
so inadequate, so unable to soothe my baby's cries, and so
depressed and resentful of my failure, my exhaustion and my lack

of achievement. Ana, my GP, asked, ever so tactfully, if I might have post-natal depression? "No, no," I answered hurriedly, "I'm just really tired."

Going back to work was unlikely to help my exhaustion (I could always try to compensate by eating more) but it might just help restore my optimism.

Some mothers are in tears over the thought of leaving their babies to return to work. Others just can't go back for a year, or more, or never. I couldn't wait to get back.

With a huge sigh of relief, I handed Art over to a childminder and returned to West Hill Surgery work for three days a week in search of a bit of cognition and self-esteem. Being a GP was something I was good at: most of my patients appreciated me. If a patient cried, I could usually soothe them and I found it easy to apply a mask of jollity, which might even remind me what an optimistic person I once was.

At least I made sure Art had a great childminder. Katrina was the captain of my squash team, who mentioned after a match that she might consider a bit of childminding now her children had gone to school. Katrina clearly was a natural – Art and she clicked from the first day. Katrina would go quite doe-eyed at how wonderful Art had been, and Art would howl when I came to collect him after work. Now that really doesn't help your self-esteem, but my self-interest overcame my jealousy. Those three days were my sanity days, and I reasoned that Art would have a nicer day with Katrina than with his grumpy, weepy mother.

Optimism Triumphing Over Experience

So why, when I clearly couldn't cope with one child, was I pregnant again? Art hadn't even turned one. Perhaps I wanted to resuscitate the lapsed optimist in me, believing that I'd do better the next time: a case of optimism triumphing over experience? Or was it because if I didn't want to subject Art to being an only child (like me), I was going to have to do it again? And I didn't want to scramble my way up from the bottom rung, only to be knocked back down.

My second pregnancy was really very easy: no diabetes, no blood pressure problems, no bleeding problems, baby growing, not even particularly sick. Just exhausted. It's quite amusing how much care and attention a mum pregnant with her first child gets, then with subsequent ones she's left to her own devices, sleep -deprived for a couple of years before she's even started, with a toddler that screams all night and gets you thrown out of a B&B, or has to be extracted from the dishwasher or the garden pond, or carted over your shoulder screaming out of the supermarket. And, oh boy, did I get porky and breathless this time, with any residual fitness and muscle tone lost having Art.

Reasons To Be Grateful. Part 12

Then Art was poorly. He was grey, he was vomiting and his liver was huge. The trouble with being a medic is that the only causes of big liver in a one year old I could think of were cancers or congenital disorders that could lead only to liver transplants or death. Suddenly nothing mattered any more. Art was in danger. I had to attend to his safety needs.

I drove him over to see my GP, feeling like a paranoid new mum. Ana was away, but her partner reassured me - I wasn't being paranoid - and sent me straight up to see the consultant. I think I would have preferred to be told I was paranoid. I staggered out of the surgery in tears, clutching Art in my arms and bumped into Vikki, the midwife.

"Em, where were you for your 24 week appoint...? Oh, Em. What's wrong?"

"I've got to take Art to hospital," I sobbed.

"Okay, give him to me. I'll help you to the car."

Over the next week, Art had scans and tests. He passed the most extraordinary white stools into his nappy, like Philadelphia cheese. Oh, God. That wasn't right, his liver must have packed up altogether. But apart from a rotavirus in his faeces specimen, everything else was negative. Dr. Smith told me rotavirus could really be very nasty sometimes, and we assumed this was the problem. Slowly Art got better. I was just so grateful for this marvellous, beautiful little being, that I had spent nearly all his life complaining about in one form or another (doesn't sleep, wouldn't breastfeed, cries all the time, wouldn't eat) to forget all the amazing things he did. Thank God Art didn't have one of these ghastly progressive genetic conditions.

That didn't last for long. My brief surge of goodwill and my thanks to God for the production and preservation of this amazing little character soon vanished with the next lost night's sleep. Oh God, and we were having another one!

Why Did Eve Have To Like Apples?

We were driving along the road last week when a pregnant sheep stood up by the fence in the corner of the field. Her belly twitched for a second or two then her lamb just dropped out of her backside. She licked her baby, then he staggered onto his feet and started suckling. How easy was that?! Why is having a baby so damned problematic for us? Well, I could blame God for committing women to an eternity of painful childbirth just because Eve fancied an apple (surely just a basic need?). But it's more to do with being too clever and evolving to stand on two legs (which I suppose is God's fault too). Standing upright tilts the pelvis forwards, forcing human babies into negotiating a complicated corner, whereas those on four legs just have a nice straight and easy birth canal (and they never get backache, either). And then the problem with all this cognition and self-actualisation is that it gives us such big heads!

Despite all my medical training and delivery of a healthy boy, I still don't understand how a head that size can ever come out such a small hole. And Art was three weeks premature. By rights, at an extra half pound a week and most first babies running over dates, I should have delivered another two pounds of baby. Urgh! Giving birth was already the closest I've ever felt to dying. It's a physiological thing, second stage fear, the huge surge of hormones needed to push that baby out. Why did God need us to feel that way? Perhaps just so we don't take the production of new life for granted? We forget how closely related birth and death can be to one another. Of course, only a hundred years ago it was death for the baby in 15 percent of cases and death for just under 1 percent of mothers. That's quite a lot, really. Now these figures are over one hundred times better.

According to Art's dinosaur book, the Triceratops had the biggest skull of any living being ... ever. But all the Mummy Triceratops had to do was lay a nice smooth egg, then put her feet up, leaving her little baby to carry on growing in the comfort of his own shell. "Right, I've done my bit, darling, it's up to you now." And she never had to breastfeed. No wonder eggs came first.

Good old evolution, eh?

Big Head Small Hole

But evolution tries to fix its own mistakes (unlike man, who breeds animals such as boxer dogs with such a big heads that they can only be born by caesarean section). Now Mother Nature has arranged for human babies to be born ever more prematurely to get round our ever-growing brains. Prehistoric woman would carry her rather less well brain-endowed baby for sixteen months, and now we are effectively having ours five months premature! No wonder we are born so pathetic that we can't even lift our (big) heads from the bed. Mind you, maybe Mother Nature isn't so daft: being pathetic forces mothers to give their babies their undivided attention for soooo much longer.

What about our own society in few hundred years time? We just can't have it that we evolve such that we can no longer be born naturally. It's okay for Mummy boxer dog as long as there's a vet on hand, but what if you're in a war situation, or the fuel supply collapses so you can't be transported to your nearest hospital, or various other apocalyptic scenarios (which do not sit well in a book by a so-called optimist). After all, we had to evacuate Serabu Hospital, which has subsequently been burnt down. So where do the women go, should they need an emergency caesarean? Best that they don't need one in the first place.

As well as giving us big heads, self-actualisation also distracts us from having our babies until we're in our thirties and beyond. And then we start demanding choice: an elective caesarean section to fit into our busy work schedules perhaps, or we go the other way and want a natural birth.

Our practice was the only one in Boldham that offered GP cover for home births. Before I had Art, I was theoretically very supportive of the idea. After I had him, I found I got a little frustrated at the doe-eyed first-time mums who would nonchalantly announce that they were having a home birth with a bit of incense and deep breathing as soon as the pregnancy test was positive. It seemed a bit disrespectful to all those mums who suffered long, painful labours, often culminating in a caesarean, to brush it off so easily. I wanted to yell "once you know what it's like, then come and ask for the next time". I was also concerned that their unrealistic expectations would leave them crushed if they ended up needing an epidural or a caesarean. Motherhood hits you right in the self esteem: guilt from the first moment. What's that all about? Then what if they struggle to breastfeed too (which I'm also sure is harder in your thirties when you're not as 'juicy', shall we say, as a teenager), already weighed down with guilt at their 'abnormal' labour? Result – they feel a total failure, when in fact they've brought a beautiful, happy, healthy, loved baby into the world and they should be feeling really, really proud of themselves for the greatest act of creation they will ever achieve.

In Praise of Teenage Pregnancy

There's nothing natural about having your first baby in your thirties (I don't remember a teenage mum ever asking for a home birth). Mother Nature wanted you to start having babies in your late teens, when you were nice and stretchy and elastic, and she probably didn't expect us to be so blooming well nourished, nor to put our feet up instead of tilling the fields until D Day. Not that I'm suggesting that we should go back to tilling the fields, but the result is ten pound babies which have to come out somehow, and that 'how' is not always through the aforesaid little hole.

Perhaps we should also stop chastising teenage mums? Frankly it's the best time to have a baby. Nice and stretchy, as I've said. And you haven't got so sucked into a young, free and single, doing-whatever-you-fancy sort of life, so that you can't adjust your expectations and feel that you're drowning in treacle when your little helpless baby arrives. But optimists don't point out problems, they come up with solutions. Smoking for all to reduce the size of the baby? Hmmm. Only if you want to reduce the baby's intelligence and future health, not to mention watching his mummy die of lung cancer. How about basic all-round education at 16, arranged marriage at 17, baby at 18? Look after it through the early years and off to college in your early twenties or perhaps thirties (depending on how many you have). You'll still have plenty of time to give to the workforce as none of us will be allowed to retire until gone seventy anyway. Perhaps grandparents could help a bit? At 17, you won't be too old to survive on no sleep and they won't be too old to help. Okay, so grandparents may not want to help, but that's how the whole continuation of the human race has managed for thousands of years. A nice, big, extended family on the doorstep. Not some mum alone in a house with a fractious baby, going slowly mad.

But enough about Western society's barbaric treatment of new mums, I was talking about caesarean sections. They can be lifesavers for baby and mum, so I'm not knocking them, I just don't want mankind to rely on them. Women feel that they are some sort of admission of defeat, which is so sad, when the reality quite often is that there was no way that the baby was coming out in one piece otherwise. A doctor friend of mine deeply, deeply regretted having her babies by caesarean. Why? She's an intelligent woman. She knows the statistics as well as I do. She was scarcely over 5ft and her babies were all over 9 pounds. It just wasn't going to happen. But when we start talking about pregnancy, labour, motherhood, all sense goes out the window. I should know; there is a lot of sense littered outside my window with bits of sense, leaving nothing but jibbering idiotdom wobbling in what's left of my grey matter.

Life Begins At Home

"Why don't you have a home birth?" suggested Di.
"What?! Me?!?"
"I promise not to tell any of your doctor pals."
So why on earth did I agree?

Eight Reasons for Having a Homebirth

1) Seemed like a nice thing to do? Nine times out of ten they go really well (and the tenth isn't generally a disaster, you just end up with a hospital birth) and of course, since I was now trying really, really hard to be an optimist, we optimists don't go around worrying about rare things that might go wrong.

2) Mums get a load more attention than a hospital birth. For starters you get an experienced midwife (two for the second stage) all to yourself, who doesn't clear off at the end of her shift or vanish to the room next door for some other mum (who might well have been more needy than you, but when you're in labour, you tend not to be feeling too magnanimous to the needs of others).

3) The research shows that they are as safe as hospital deliveries if you select appropriate people to have them, and I was a pretty appropriate person, second baby, normal delivery for the first, sensible (?) mum, decent-sized, clean (?) bedroom, telephone and striking distance to the nearest hospital in the case of disaster.

4) The pethidine I was given for Art when I arrived at the hospital (after a horrible, nauseating, uncomfortable journey) didn't touch the pain, it just made me sick again, so I might as well have been at home. At least I wouldn't vomit over someone's Jimmy Choos on the journey in.

5) The Boldham midwives were really positive and experienced with home births.

6) Because I made such a hash of breastfeeding Art, I wanted to re-establish my credentials. And my self-esteem.

7) When Art screamed in the hospital, no one took him away, not even for a second, so I got no sleep at all. At least at home Danny, or a grandparent or a friend might take him downstairs for a jiggle and let me have a nap without a cleaner coming in to change my jug of water/the bin or a consultant do their ward round etc., etc., etc.

8) I remembered a home birth I attended with a surrogate mum, the surrogate mum's husband, the genetic mum, the genetic Dad and two midwives all crammed into the front bedroom of a Boldham semi, with four flutes and a bottle of champagne cooling on the bedside table ready to be cracked open at the moment of delivery. Never mind Danny leaving me in hospital and going home to toast our baby's head, *I* wanted to toast my baby's head. So glugging down the champers within an hour of the birth did it for me!

Em Doesn't Feel Like Fish and Chips

It took me some time to decide I was actually in labour as I had been having Braxton Hicks contractions, or practice pains, for weeks. At first I thought they were psychosomatic as it was a bit early and Danny was going away for a stag weekend trail biking. Lucky sod. His parents, Peg and Bob, and brother Mick who was ever so good with Art, were staying to help me. I bleeped Di and left a message on her answering machine. Was it today or tomorrow she was coming back from holiday? I couldn't remember, so I bleeped Vikki and left a message on her answering machine too. Fair enough, it was the weekend. I waited for a bit to see if either Di or Vikki would get back to me. Then I had a 'show' – the mucous plug coming away from the cervix as it opens up. Yes, I was definitely in labour. My in-laws are perfectly fine, but I really didn't fancy having them in the house whilst I gave birth, so I suggested to Peg and Bob that they take Art home with them for the weekend.

"No problem," they said, and popped out to get fish and chips. Er, I meant *now*. There was no word from Di or Vikki, so it was time to get in the backup troops. I phoned Delivery Ward for the on call midwife.

"The on call midwife is out on another delivery."

"Okay, well what about the second on call?"

Oh, yes, okay, they could call her. Then Danny got a call from a long lost friend in Belgium and was nattering on the phone for over half an hour. I decided to play it cool and sat down to eat the fish and chips. No. Couldn't.

"Better go, John, my wife thinks she's in labour." Danny finally hung up and came in the kitchen. He saw my untouched bag of fish and chips. "You haven't eaten anything, you must be in labour! Looks like I'm not going for my trail riding after all."

Still no call from a midwife. Perhaps she'd been trying to get through when Danny was on the phone. I phoned back. Oh yes, there was a note about it here. They'd try again to get someone. I put the phone down and then my waters went, pushing the contractions way up the Richter scale.

The phone rang. It was the second on-call midwife, who said that she'd get there when the first on call midwife needed her in second stage (that's the actual pushing the baby out bit).

Oh. Okay. I put the phone down. "But the first on call isn't here!" I suddenly realised (not thinking very clearly). Still trying to play it cool, I helped Danny put the plastic sheeting on the bed, then packed a little overnight bag for Art, and twiddled aimlessly with the TENS machine. It was getting to be bloody sore and I suddenly felt very weak and pathetic. I had to lie down. The phone rang. It was Vikki back from her shopping. I could hear Danny.

"Yes, yes...waters gone...contractions every two minutes, yes, she's had a show...getting quite painful. Fine."

"Vikki says she'll come when you're in second stage," Danny called over from the phone.

"But there's nobody here!" I howled from the bed.

Okay. Vikki was coming. Shit. I wanted to push. Oh, not yet. What if it was a shoulder dystocia, or an undiagnosed breech? It's hard to be an optimist when you're in pain. Epicurus believed we should avoid pain. Yes, yes, I think so too. If I'd gone to hospital I could have an epidural. What a dumb idea having a home birth! I didn't care how many shoes I vomited over. I heard a car door slam and an engine starting. No that was the wrong way round. That was Peg, Bob and Mick leaving, not a midwife coming. I was starting to panic, why had I been so stupid? Why hadn't I gone to hospital? My baby was going to die, I was going to die, we were both going to...

"Okay, Em, you're doing fine. Just breathe and relax."

And that voice of a total stranger in a blue dress really helped. I felt safe, and, with my safety needs fulfilled, I knew it would all be alright. "Would you like some gas and air?"

"YES PLEASE!"

But it never appeared – some problem with the new cylinder valve. Not that I remembered it being particularly effective. I pushed and broke Danny's fingers instead. Then Vikki appeared, and then Baby Frank appeared! No stitches. Vikki helped me put Frankie to the breast and he sucked, no trouble at all. Within 20 minutes, I was in the bath whilst the midwives scooped up all the gubbins and placentas and things in the plastic sheet, and within fifty minutes I was drinking champagne with Danny. Another peak experience. In fact the whole of Maslow's hierarchy in an hour. Safety, self-esteem and basic needs (he breastfed!), love and belonging, the pain stopped, a baby appeared and self-actualisation. The bit of virtue thrown in was letting Danny go for his trail biking weekend after all.

My pal Sam came round to baby and mummy sit (good excuse for a bit more champagne!) And I even got some sleep that night.

Life's a miracle! Have I said that before?

10. Family Life.

A Series of Accidents Colliding Under One Roof

"Life is an object with a definite boundary, continually exchanging material with its environment." Encyclopedia Britannica

"Accidents will happen in the best regulated families." Dickens. David Copperfield (1850)

"Go with the flow." Lao-Tzu (founder of Taoism, 2,000 years ago), paraphrased a little

Expectation Management

In the early days with Art, Danny would say, "Let's just get through the day with all of us in one piece. Anything else is a bonus." But Frankie was different. What a great little baby! He nuzzled up and breastfed beautifully and, after eight weeks of two hourly feeds, he slept from 9.30pm – 5.30am. Wow! *Breast is Best* said that the hormones released in breastfeeding have a feel-good effect and help you sleep, and I think it was true. I was really quite relaxed (for me) and happy and (surprise, surprise) was rather enjoying being a mum. Perhaps I had finally accepted that my needs would be secondary for the time being. I would take a leaf out of Lao-Tzu's book of Tao: *The Tao is The Way and everything moves from non being to being to non being. Allow the Tao to flow unchallenged and the world becomes a tranquil place*. Okay. I would go with the flow. (It's always easier to be philosophical when you're looking after a baby who doesn't scream).

Frankie did wonders for Art. When Peg and Bob brought him back, Art marched straight over to his little brother, not yet a day old, sleeping peacefully in his carry cot and announced BABY! Art's first ever word. See, even a relatively new life is impressed with new life. Art, always Mr. Competitive, even at 18 months, must have realized there was a new babe on the block, and that he had better start impressing us with the next stage. And impress us he did.

Grandpa John is a Genius

Having small children may put your self-actualisation on hold whilst you concentrate on their bottom rung needs, but boy oh boy, your children go galloping up the pyramid leaving you to watch in weary wonderment.

All Art's words must have been just crouching in his frontal lobes, for by the end of the week fifty or more pounced out, and within the month they were in lovely little sentences. (Dr. Maslow, you've got to put speech somewhere on your pyramid, it's just so dammed impressive).

We were going to visit Grandpa John and Grandma Kat. Grandpa John does not find children sweet, amusing, nor impressive. Obviously this had to be rectified. My first sentence was apparently 'Daddy is a Genius' so we taught Art to say 'Grandpa John is a genius'. Our mission: to get Art to make Grandpa John smile. (Not that my Dad is a sourpuss; he has a great sense of humour. It's just the children thing. Perhaps that's why I'm not a natural at motherhood. I'm just genetically unsuited for it. Bit late now).

Anyway, Grandpa John was doing The Times crossword in the porch when we arrived. Art, not quite two, marched in and announced, "Grandpa John is a genius!" And The Times slipped, just enough to reveal what was surely a smile.

"What about 'Daddy is a genius'. Can you say that, Art?" Danny suggested hopefully.

Art thought about this one for a minute. "No ..." he said. "Daddy's not a genius. Grandpa John is a genius."

"Oh," said Danny. "Okay." And Grandpa John's newspaper positively shook.

A few months later my parents visited us in Bolham and we thought we'd try the 'getting Art to make Grandpa John to smile' trick again.

"Who's a genius, Art?"

No reply. Oh, what a pity. He'd probably forgotten.

"Art, who's a genius?" I asked. Silence. "Is Daddy a genius?"

"No."

"Is Grandpa John a genius?" Art shook his head. "Is anyone a genius, Art?"

Art considered the question carefully and replied. "Art's a genius!"

And Grandpa John beamed. He could see his little grandson was of his line.

That night at bedtime, Art went round and gave everyone a goodnight kiss. Grandma Peg, Granddad Bob, Uncle Mick, Mummy, Daddy, Grandma Kat and Baby Frank. All duly kissed. Then he arrived at Grandpa John's chair. Grandpa John was never big on kisses. There was an awkward pause as grandson and Grandpa eyed each other suspiciously. What to do? Finally my Dad broke the deadlock by holding out his hand. And he and the two year old shook hands. Perfect. Art giggled and sprinted up to bed.

Donald Duck

Frank just smiled, gurgled and fed, being the perfect baby who just idolized his older brother. But he was not to be outdone on the race up the pyramid. Frankie's party piece was to quack like Donald Duck. The first time, we were walking the dogs by the river with eleven month old Frankie in my backpack when a duck waddled past quacking: 'Wwwhquack, wwwhquack'. And from my shoulder a perfect 'whhhquack whhhquack' came in reply.

For that brief moment I don't think I would have minded if I never slept or saw a bar of chocolate again.

"How does a duck go, Frank?" we would ask, over and over again. "How does a duck go?" And Frank would 'wwwhquack wwwhquack' obligingly, leaving us chortling helplessly every time.

I took him on a house-call to one of my elderly patients. Frank spotted a duck on her teatray and started wwwhquacking frantically. My patient just howled with laughter – so much better than antidepressants. Every doctor should have a Frankie.

But life moves on. Children grow up and they develop. One day we asked Frank "How does a duck go?" and Frankie said "Quack quack" in perfectly enunciated English. I should have been pleased at my boy's development, I should have been glad he'd reached the next stage, but instead I cried. They grow up so fast.

Frankie started walking before he was 11 months. My delight at my baby being so precocious, SO advanced, SO clever ('you mean little Dick isn't walking yet? Oh well, there's nothing to worry about, they all do it in their own time') soon evaporated as I now had a baby under one, and a toddler not yet three, sprinting off (and upward where possible) in opposite directions. All this development, this proto self-actualisation, this independence was great, but it was bloody exhausting, not to mention jeopardising their safety needs. Didn't they understand that little boys are supposed to cling to their mother's apron strings? Maybe if I'd ever worn an apron and stood helpfully by the kitchen sink...?

Childcare, the Working Mum's Cross

I had been begging to get back to work after I had Art, just to feel like myself again, and do something I was actually good at, rather than fumbling my way through motherhood. However, Frank was such a sweetie and Art so much easier now we could speak to each other, that going back to work the second time was a bit of a wrench. It also left the ghastly childcare problem as Katrina felt she really couldn't manage my scatty schedule with two children. Nanny No. 1 left after four months for the lights of London. Nanny No. 2 was pregnant by the second month and vomited profusely for three months, leaving me repeatedly stranded with two little boys under three, a surgery full of patients booked for 8.30am and Danny in London. Peg and Bob came over when they could, but Peg was marooned on a waiting list to get her knee replaced, and was really in too much pain to be chasing hyper-active toddlers. Fortunately the receptionists, practice manager, practice nurse and cleaner at West Hill Surgery were all very good with children. We booked the boys into nursery, but because of the short notice, they were in two different nurseries, with Katrina covering some of the slack. The boys loved nursery, Art depleting the world's paper resources with his drawings and Frankie turning on his big dimpled grin to all the little girls who chorused: 'Hi Frankie' as he sat down for hot toast.

One day there was a note on the door of Frank's nursery: Closed until further notice. Some problem with the nursery manager not following rules and regulations. So once more the staff of West Hill Surgery had to become creative with specimen pots and waiting room toys.

The nursery reopened a couple of weeks later with a new manager. But there was no more hot toast. Tellingly, Frank hesitated at the door. Talk about children having a second sense. It closed a couple of weeks after that. Still don't know what it was all about. We finally got Frank into a new nursery, not Art's one (full), but yet another one, that Frank called 'Harry's nursery' (our next door neighbour's little boy) and Harry's nursery it remained for the next two years.

Donald Duck Loses His Girlfriend

Danny was working in Heathrow, leaving me alone during the week and exhausted with the boys, part-time work and ramshackle childcare. Self-actualisation no longer even crossed my mind. Meanwhile Danny was exhausted with full-time work and the long weekly commute. We spent a lot of time arguing who was the more exhausted, thus exhausting ourselves even more.

Once or twice I would take the boys to London, rather than Danny commuting up to Boldham. *Disney Fantasia 2000* was on at the Imax cinema. The London Imax is a big, circular structure, with doors all round, in the middle of a roundabout at Waterloo. We were queuing into the auditorium with 18 month Frankie and three year old Art. Suddenly there was no Art. We looked all round, in the toilets, round the corridor, up and down the stairs. Danny spoke to the staff, who let him announce over the loudspeakers: "Has anyone seen a three year old boy? ... Art, it's Daddy here, where are you?" Nothing. Danny dashed in and out of every bloody one of the automatic doors at the Imax, and up and down the roads and subways filing out from each entrance. I clutched Frank and walked round and round and round inside, hoping Art would suddenly appear. All parents probably have lost a child at some time, and you start off cool, thinking they'll appear, then panicky, but manage to control it, then move on to straight-out frightened. Safety. Our basic need that we never really think about. God, you've got to look after your children. Finally they made another announcement over the tannoy. "Has anybody seen a three-year old boy in a red and green anorak?"

"Oh, yes," said a lady, "Now you mention it, there's a little boy sitting next to me, watching the film."

And there Art was, happily engrossed with Mickey Mouse.

"Art, darling. Didn't you hear Daddy?" I sobbed. "On the loudspeaker?"

"Oh yes, I heard Daddy's voice," said Art. "So I knew I was all right!"

Fantasia 2000 has a sequence about Noah's Ark. All the animals are boarding in their couples, leaving a lone Donald Duck searching desperately for his girlfriend, because if she doesn't get on board she'll be lost in the flood water forever. And ... oh no, it's making me cry again. Finally Donald climbs up the Ark's gangway, totally dejected (and cartoons do dejected very well) then he turns the corner, the tears in his eyes and ... Whoopee!

There she was! She'd been on the Ark all the time! Well, I sat in the Imax with my lost and found son, sobbing my heart out over Donald Duck and his lost girlfriend.

Now, I have a bit of a problem with God over the whole Noah's Ark thing. The Prodigal Son, that's a much better story. I want to believe God forgives his children and looks after their safety. I want to believe He's a better, more patient parent than I, never shouting at his children. He certainly doesn't drown them all, just because they are a bit naughty. I'll accept that some chap called Noah was around during a nasty flood and he did his best to rescue what beasts and livestock he could in his Ark, and without satellite TV, as far as Noah was concerned, his whole world would have been flooded. Possibly he embellished the story a little to the bible reporter (who must have been on the Ark too) as he did come out of it rather well. Anyway, the more animals you have under your care, the more likely you are to lose a few. Ditto with small children, and I only had two!

I Don't Want to be a Dinosaur

That was just a tiny safety scare, which I mention just to remind us how tenacious our grip on safety really is on this planet. As well as Donald Duck and Mickey Mouse, *Fantasia* has a scene depicting the extinction of the dinosaurs with great red landscapes of dying dinosaurs turning first to skeletons, and then to dust.

A very impressive piece of animation, but was that something we should take our babies to see, just because we fancied a bit of entertainment? Self-actualisation, knowledge, aesthetics whatever, is all very fine, but there's also over-stimulation. That night, Art tossed and turned, asleep in bed, aged three, crying out: "But I don't want to be a dinosaur!"

I don't really want to be a dinosaur either, darling, for all their size. Not much self-actualisation going on Jurassic times, but then how would we really know? I hear that some mavericks think the T-Rex was a wimpy scavenger instead of the world's greatest ever predator, and that dinosaurs may have been hot blooded after all. Phil, if he was still with us, probably wouldn't believe that dinosaurs ever existed in the first place: just some baked bones, like the baked basalt to fake moon rock, to create the huge dinosaur industry. Oh dear, I seem to be talking about dinosaurs again. Forgive me. But anyone with little boys will know that dinosaurs feature highly on the agenda of daily life, so they have lumbered into my consciousness.

We think of dinosaurs as being failures for committing the heinous crime of extinction (if you exclude their grand evolutionary development into chickens), but they lived for 17 million years. We humans have only been around for 2 million years, and looking at our 'progress' 2,000,100 is looking a bit dodgy. Sorry. I'm supposed to be an optimist, but I don't want my children to face extinction. Of course what happens to my children is of no great import to the continuation of life (a fact I'll probably never accept) but if they don't survive a nuclear holocaust or a meteorite colliding with Earth, you can bet there's some tencacious little bacterium or cockroach who will. There's always something else to climb out of the primordial soup. And, having forgotten to take my contraceptive pills to Strathfarrell for the annual Christmas gathering at Monikie, it would seem that there was going to be another little pikelet crawling out of our own soup.

11. The Value of Life

Life Is Priceless. Life Is Cruel.

Is a Cockroach Worth It?

Why is it that we aren't very happy with the idea of cockroaches inheriting the Earth?

Well, life is a hierarchy, or at least, we love to give things a value and an order and we humans naturally put ourselves at the top. Someone, somewhere, seems to have given themselves the job of assigning values to a life's worth. For instance, Kings and Queens, at the top (whether from some quirk of birth, or possibly singing or footballing ability), assorted lesser mortals spreading out in a pyramid below, possibly not so often by class these days, but certainly by income, with the occasional low income aberration (e.g.: Ghandi, Mother Theresa), who sneaks in by sheer exceptionality and thus fame. And of course we in the West consider ourselves so much more valuable than those from anywhere else. Am I being too cynical for an optimist again? But why else is the life of a Sri Lankan man worth so much less than a Western tourist? Because they are worth less in monetary terms? So we end up with a hierarchy based on:

- Wealth
- Fame
- Age (generally losing value when you get older),
- Sex (depending where you live – women and children first off The Titanic, for instance. You see, now I've got boys, I

have suddenly started worrying about the fate of men. Most of the time, and most places, I'll admit, it's a man's world)
- Intelligence, or at least marketable skills
- Health (losing value as you lose health, especially if you should have mental health problems, no matter how transitory)
- Other people in developed countries who speak English
- Other people in developed countries who don't speak English
- Those in developing countries, in a sub-hierarchy according to wealth and influence.

Then down to the rest of the Kingdom of Life:
- Animals are worth more than vegetables (and the Jains, for instance, have hierarchies of vegetables)
- Mammals more worthy than fish
- Fish more worthy than crustaceans and arachnids
- Crustaceans and arachnids worth more than insects (gets a bit dodgy here, personally I'd prefer a bee to a cockroach. Spiders are good because they eat flies, but I'm not so keen on the poisonous, frightening ones that might kill me)
- Insects a notch above parasites
- And parasites somehow superior to bacteria (although someone is not awarding enough points to those magnificent blue-green algae!)

I, like all of us, have my own hierarchy:
- Me
- My children
- Danny
- Other family (mine)
- Best friends
- Other family (in-laws)
- Good friends (I'll include virtual acquaintances here. I've found myself a really cool American email friend for instance)
- Friends

- Colleagues (some are, or certainly working towards, the friend category)
- My patients
- Acquaintances (and they have their own hierarchy according to e.g.: if they are friendly, or say they've read my book!)
- Strangers who appear to have something in common with me
- Other strangers I deem worthy in some way
- Strangers (people) who I know nothing about
- Animals (in their own hierarchy according to cuteness or beauty)
- Plants
- People I consider unworthy.

That last one sounds very judgmental, but I mean really unworthy, like Ghenghis Khan, Hitler, Stalin, Pol Phot, not just Katie Trollope who thinks my children are out of control (irritating because she's right), or mean, like those girls who abandoned me in a hotel in India (if you are reading this, no, you are not forgiven).

The trouble with being judgmental is that you usually won't have all the information. For instance, I've just read an article saying that although Ghenghis committed all sorts of atrocities, he was clearly a military genius, promoting his troops on merit, not breeding, and was the first civilisation to give equal rights to women.

Of course, there are some blurring of categories. Should Danny's mum take precedence to my best friend Sam? And what about Bo? Family, best friend, good friend, friend or just at the top of the animal category? Given a direct choice by a kidnapper of my dog or an unknown child, I'd choose the child, but in real life, that situation is unlikely to occur. I could save several children a year in Sierra Leone for the money we spend on dog food, vets bills and replacement Christmas turkeys and sausages.

How does all this tally with the state of our NHS? Should we pay for the most up to date kidney machine or the very best chemotherapy for a child? It's difficult. That kidney machine could pay for thousands, hundreds of thousands, of children to be vaccinated 'elsewhere', or for thousands of simple lifesaving operations, or hundreds of water wells to be built. Every human life is precious, but some are more precious than others? And other life forms are not precious at all? So we should pay for chemotherapy for a boy, but not to save a species from existence? Even if that species happened to be, say, blue-green algae, one of the lowest forms of life? I don't know. If every life is precious, shouldn't we do whatever it takes to sustain it? Well yes, if it's a member of your own family...

Receptionist Rage

There is a tendency to assume that the physical difficulties of people with any history of a mental health problem are psychosomatic. Like Mick's sore throat, then his difficulty swallowing, then his trouser belt having no more notches left to tighten. My brother-in-law made ever more regular appearances at his GP, who prescribed several multi-coloured antibiotic capsules, and when Mick said he couldn't swallow them, his GP prescribed the antibiotics in syrup form.

If anybody had told me, I would have intervened earlier, but they probably didn't tell me because I'd made it quite clear I thought it inappropriate to be giving medical care for my extended family's health problems. And I was pregnant again – an excuse to focus entirely on myself and my baby and relinquish all responsibility for the health of the world, the health of my patients and the health of everyone else, including, as it turned out, the health of my other children.

When Danny did mention Mick's difficulty swallowing and appended it with the words 'for six months', I was horrified. Why hadn't Mick been referred? Why hadn't he told his GP? Why hadn't anyone said anything to me?

Difficulty swallowing in a smoker (not including the transient trouble you might get with a painful sore throat) is cancer until proved otherwise, and one of the few improvements in the new look NHS is the 'two week rule', where alarm bell symptoms are supposed to be referred and seen within the fortnight. I went to see Mick, me blossoming in heavy pregnancy and Mick, thin, drawn and cachectic.

"Mick! How much weight have you lost?"

"Three stones. Well I can't swallow, can I, so it's hardly surprising."

Three stones! God. "Did you tell your GP? Has he referred you?"

"He said he'd referred me to a specialist about six weeks ago."

"Six weeks? So when's your appointment?"

"I haven't heard back."

"What? Not a letter with a date, or a phone call?"

Bloody hell. It didn't seem helpful to say "What a cock-up and you've probably got cancer and your GP's just been ignoring it because you've had a few problems in the past." Instead I said. "I'll phone the hospital and try and find out what's happened."

"Ear Nose and Throat. Mick Pike? No...sorry, we haven't got that referral yet...oh, yes actually we have. The consultant has re-routed it to the swallow clinic."

That was good. A specialist swallow clinic suggested there should be a specialist interested specifically in swallowing.

"Swallow clinic, can I help you? No, Mick Pike hasn't got an appointment. The letter hasn't been marked urgent."

"Er, sorry, but isn't dysphasia always urgent?"

"Just a minute, there's a note here. Yes. The Consultant, Mr. J., has looked at the letter himself and said that Mr. Pike obviously needs an endoscopy. Mr. J. has listed him directly for endoscopy rather than have him wait for an outpatient appointment. To save time. Shall I put you through to endoscopy?"

"Thanks."

"Endoscopy clinic. Mick Pike? Yes, he's quite near the top of the list."

"Good. Have you got an appointment date?"

"Well, no. He'll be one of the first to get one as soon as the endoscopy clinic is reopened."

"Excuse me? Reopened?"

"The endoscopy clinic has been closed for refurbishment for six weeks now. It should only be another couple of weeks."

"Er, surely Mr. J. would have known that endoscopy would be closed."

"Well it's taken a bit longer than we..."

"It always does. Anyway, we can't wait 'a couple of weeks', Mick obviously needs an urgent outpatient appointment while he's waiting for endoscopy. Mr. J. could be doing something else, a barium swallow, or a scan, or do an endoscopy in theatre for heavens sake. Mick can't even swallow his beer!"

"Well you'll have to re-refer him."

"Right."

I did tell the first lady on my little loop that I was Mick's sister-in-law and not his GP, but had rather lost patience on telephone call number three. I phoned Mick's GP. The receptionist rather sniffily said that Dr. F. couldn't divulge any confidential information to strangers.

"Well, you're right, but I'm not a stranger, I'm Mick's sister-in-law and I don't want Dr. F. to divulge any information to me. *I* want to divulge some information to Dr. F."

"What information?"

Information that if Dr. F. had been doing his job properly in the first place he would know already. Anyway, I don't want to divulge confidential information to you either, you snotty cow.

(Well, that's not how the conversation went at all, I'm far too polite for that, but that's what I felt like. I was obviously going to have to use my 'I'm a GP card' which I always try hard not to because I expect people to be civil anyway.)

"Please, I'd like to talk to Dr. F. about Mick. I'm a GP and he's my brother-in-law and we're all very concerned about him. There's a problem with his referral that Dr. F. needs to know about."

"He's busy."

"Can he ring back?"

"He's got surgery this afternoon."

"I'm sure he could give me five minutes beforehand."

"He's very busy." God, this woman! The receptionists at my surgery were always lovely. (Must remember to tell them that). What was wrong with her?

"When's a good time for me to ring back?"

"I suppose you could try about three."

"Thank you."

I rang at 2.59. Busy. 3.10. Busy. 3.30. Busy.

"Perhaps he could ring me when he's free? I feel it's quite urgent."

As a doctor I hated being hassled by pushy patients, so I tried to give my colleague a little respect. I waited in. I arranged for friends to collect Art from school. He never rang. I rang at 5.45. Dr. F. had gone home. Lazy, inconsiderate, incompetent ... or perhaps it was that snotty receptionist who never gave him the message? I am not by nature an aggressive person, but I was starting to understand road rage, or indeed receptionist rage.

"Perhaps you could ask Dr. F. to ring me tomorrow?" I asked sweetly.

I told Mick all about the endoscopy and the need for another referral, and told him to make another appointment with Dr. F. I wrote it all down in a letter to give to Mick to deliver himself, and put a copy to Dr. F in the post.

Dr. F never rang the next day, and was out at a meeting or on visits on the three times I called. Mick did say he'd seen Dr. F the next day and that Dr. F said he'd look into it. Fine. I really wanted to trust a colleague. Another week passed and there was still no word. I was going to ring again but then Frankie was poorly, and in my defence my in-laws come below my children.

12. Womb With A View.

Life in Utero

"...twinkle, twinkle little star, how I wonder what I am...like a diamond in Mummy's tum....only four days until I come."

Oh, hello. I'm...well I don't know if I'm an Ella Margaret or Stuart Robert yet. It's dark in here and Mummy didn't ask at the scan. She didn't like to spoil the surprise. Let's have a little feel. Hmmm, yes...boy, I think...no, no, that's my finger. Just a minute, yes, definitely boy. No, umbilical cord. Never mind, only four days before we find out.

Four days!!!! It's so exciting I can hardly breathe. Oh, all right, I can't breathe yet, but we babies do make a few practice breaths.

Mummy says only three percent of babies arrive on the day they are supposed to, but I'm all set, head down and ready for action to make sure I'm one of them. It's a family thing: Daddy was born on the first of April (Mummy thinks that's funny), Uncle Rod the first of January and big brother Art on the first of February. Frank was supposed to be the first of August but was, as usual, over-eager, and came a week early, so it's down to me, Baby Pike III to arrive on the first of October.

All Mummy's patients keep saying. "Two boys, eh, you'll be wanting a girl then?"

"No, no," she says. "I really don't mind." Liar! We are connected so I know exactly what she's thinking and she'd love me to be a girl. Now this is a bit of a worry. What if I'm a boy? Huh! Then what? Not much I can do about it, is there? "Just as long as they sleep," Mummy usually adds, as a little joke to make her patients laugh. Mummy's got this idea that girls are going to be well-behaved and sleep through the night from the very first day, not play with the knives in the drawers, or the poisons in the cupboards, wee in the potty and not in the pants, sit ever so quietly doing drawing in the corner and do something called the ironing. So much for girl power. To be fair to Mummy, Art and Frank are exhausting, and that's just from in here. They laugh, they shout, they lose slugs in supermarkets, they jump off they furniture and they bounce off the bed and on top of me and I'm not even born yet. So here's the deal. If I'm a boy, I'll be ever so good. Honest. But boy, oh boy, if I'm a girl I'm going to create holy hell! Ha! Hope I'm a girl.

Oh, here comes my favourite song:

"...Hey, hey-yeh baybay. Ooob! Ah! I wanna know-oh-oh-oh-oh oh, if you'll be my girl." Yes I will. I'll be your girl, Mummy! Or your boy. We're dancing. Well, I'm not dancing exactly, I'm being bounced up and down and I am kicking my legs. There's not much else I can do with my arms folded and my head jammed into Mummy's pelvis.

Time out! Toilet break. Oh Mummy, sit down a bit more carefully, I've just banged the back of my head against your pubic ramus. Not much wee came out, did it? Why don't you do as Di suggested and sit facing the cistern, then you might get a better flow and we won't have to come again five minutes later. Mummy won't though. Sit facing the cistern, I mean. Come on, you're about to have a baby (me!), there's no point suddenly pretending you've got standards. Am I complaining about having to wee straight into my amniotic fluid? No. Doesn't sound great, but that's what we babies do. Like astronauts. And astronauts are prime examples of vitality, health and self-actualisation, even if Phil, that patient of Mummy's, was right and they never landed on the moon. Whatever 'vitality', 'self-actualisation' and the 'moon' are. Mummy uses some funny words sometimes, but I thought I'd just try them out. Get a bit of a head start for when I start talking in two years time.

Mummy keeps saying she's an optimist and optimists aren't worriers. So why is she worrying about me? Baby's are natural unborn optimists, but what with Mummy getting it into her head that something's going to go wrong, now even I've started worrying about my health. I feel fine, but it's dark in here, so who knows if I have an extra leg or am covered in spots? Mummy's got two perfectly healthy (if extremely noisy) little boys and she says they were no trouble in pregnancy and that they came out easily enough, so now she thinks it will be third time unlucky. Meaning what? Hey, I don't want to have a horrible delivery, get cut off from my placenta or strangled by the cord or get my shoulders stuck when my head's out. My brain isn't very developed yet, but it's got loads of potential – Great Granny Jane got a first in maths and physics, Great Granddad Ahcong was a solicitor, Grandpa John is awfully good at crosswords, and Granddad Bob and Uncle Rod can make anything out of anything. Okay, so Mummy did drink the occasional glass of wine when no one was watching, but she's never smoked and she did take her folic acid and even started swallowing those LCP omega-3 fatty acids.

So if Mummy thinks something is bound to go wrong, why oh why is she going to have me at home? Her doctor friends think it's a terrible idea. At least I know Frank was born at home, and although Frankie can't count to ten in French and German yet, like two year old Suzy Smith, he can build a lego tanker in five minutes, which is reassuring. And according to Mummy, with his smile it won't matter if Frankie never counts to ten in French or German. Anyway, we babies are supposed to be optimists. There's absolutely no reason I shouldn't just slide out easily: she's a big girl, my Mummy.

Mummy always qualifies not minding if I'm a boy or a girl with "just as long as it's healthy". So what if I'm not healthy, huh? Spina bifida, Downs, or cerebral palsy or something? Won't that do? Maybe it's not supposed to be dark in here, oh no, maybe I'm blind! Calm down, calm down. If I'm blind, it'll be just like in here and in here's really rather nice. Warm, velvet black, with a gentle whoosh, whoosh, whoosh. Until the brothers jump on me, or she falls down the steps at the swimming pool, or flat on her belly as she chased Frankie who was trying to ring the church bell in the middle of the service. She seems to be doing that sort of thing quite a lot. Accident-prone. She blames it on me for upsetting her centre of balance. What about the skiing holiday when I was only 12 weeks, Mummy? I ask you, what sort of doctor is she? Black runs, *vin chaud*, and she even polished off a blue cheese salad, before remembering she was pregnant. Oh no. I'm going to be deformed!

Only two days to D Day now, but she doesn't seem to be thinking about me any more. Uncle Mick is poorly in Hedon, and Frankie is poorly on the sofa. Mummy's spent all day on the phone, first to Grandma Peg and Granddad Bob, who were worried that Mick is losing so much weight, then to the doctor people who are supposed to be looking after Uncle Mick. I thought 'losing weight' was a good thing as Mummy is always saying she needs to do it, but when they talk about Mick, it seems to be a big problem. Just as well Frank has spent most of the day asleep, so she could make all those phone calls.

I might as well go to sleep too. I've got my big entrance to make.

Yawn. Good morning. Or is it good night? Hard to tell. Hmmm. I feel a bit funny, is something wrong? Mummy and Daddy are talking about phoning the doctor. What? Is it me? Are they worried about me? Is there a problem? Oh, no. Please let me be healthy. I want to be perfect. I give a few kicks, but Mummy doesn't notice. It's Frank they're talking about. Phew! Sorry, selfish, I know, but all the psychology books say we babies can only ever think of ourselves. I try to stretch, but there's no room. Mummy's talking, very slowly. That's strange. Mummy never talks slowly. She's saying that Frankie's a good colour and his temperature's down and his breathing is fine and that he probably just needs to sleep it off. Daddy seems quite happy with this. Mummy's the doctor, and she sounds quite calm. But she isn't calm at all. I've just realised that's why I feel funny, it's all that adrenaline. Look, Mummy, you're just not making it clear to Daddy how worried you are, even if you don't really know why you're worried. Daddy's not worried because he thinks you're not that worried, so tell him how worried you are.

"I'm sure Frankie'll be fine by morning," she's saying. "He's just weak because he hasn't eaten."

No, no, no, Mummy, you know, you know there's something wrong. *I* know there's something wrong and I'm not even born yet.

"I'll sleep by Frankie's bed," says Daddy. "You need to get some sleep, you've got the baby to think of."

About time someone remembered me.

Bringgg bringgg, bringgg bringg. "What on ea...? Maybe I'll be blind but I'm not going to be deaf. What was that? Oh yes. Alarm clock. Mummy said she'd get up at three to check Frank. Good colour, temperature down, all nice and peaceful. See Mummy, no need to worry at all. Now you can put all that adrenaline back where it came from and let us both have a nice night's sleep.

They can't wake him up! It's eight o'clock and they can't wake him up. That's bad. I know that's bad. Daddy carries Frankie downstairs.

"Frankie? Darling? Darling?" Mummy's shaking Frank. "Oh, no. Danny, I can't wake him up. Frankie? Frankie darling?"

I've never heard Mummy like this before. All panicky. But she tries very hard to be calm. "Can you take Art over to Katrina's? Ask if she'll take him to school?" she asks Daddy "I'll ring Ana."

She's pressing all the wrong numbers for the doctor. She tries again and gets through.

"It's Em Pike, I'm sorry to ring so early, but can I speak to a doctor urgently? I can't wake my little boy up."

She speaks very slowly and very calmly. Too slow and too calm. Otherwise the receptionist might have ordered an ambulance rather than saying she'd get one of the doctors to phone as soon as they got in.

"Okay."

No, Mummy, not okay. We sit next to Frankie and try to talk to him, sing to him, get him to say something or move, or groan or anything. Not okay, Mummy. It doesn't matter that his pulse and breathing and temperature are all fine, and that he doesn't have a rash, or neck stiffness, or that he's not cold and clammy. He's unconscious, Mummy! And I'm just telling you what you are telling me. Phone an ambulance. Drive him to Casualty.

"What did the doctor say?" Daddy's asking from the front door.

"They're not in yet, it's just gone eight...oh, there's the phone."

"Ana, I'm so glad it's you. Frankie's unconscious, we can't... no, no. Yes, thanks. No, we'll take him straight to Paeds. No, I'm sure we don't need an ambulance. It'll probably be quicker if we take him directly."

Yes, you do need an ambulance, Mummy, for heavens sake! She's being too calm again, otherwise Daddy would have grabbed the phone out of her hand and called for an ambulance himself. To make matters worse, she drives because she says it means Daddy can carry Frank up to the ward whilst she tries to park. Talk about dangerous drivers! A pregnant mother, sleep deprived, trying not to panic, obviously thinking very unclearly, at rush hour with no blue light and no siren and no oxygen, who's due to give birth at any moment.

Okay, Mummy, never mind the October the first thing. I think I'd better stay in here for a bit longer.

13. For Dear Life

"All shall be well, and all shall be well, and all manner of thing shall be well." St. Juliana of Norwich (1342-1423)

They won't let me in to CT scanning. Why won't they let me in with Frankie? Then I remember. I'm pregnant. Very pregnant. So I sit on a plastic chair in the empty corridor as the scanning room door shuts behind my little boy. How could I have let this happen? How could I have failed so totally, both as Frank's mother and as a doctor? I knew he wasn't right last night. I knew; I could feel it. But he had no stiff neck, or rash, and he'd been talking to me before he went to bed. Even though his temperature was down and his colour good and his breathing normal, he just wasn't right. Frankie just wasn't right, and now he's in CT scanning, within an hour of arriving at the hospital, with a Glasgow Coma Score of three. You can't get any lower than that without being brain dead and no-one gets a CT scan for months unless it's drastic. And they took him straight here. Within the hour. Children usually need to be sedated to keep them absolutely still for the thirty minutes it takes to do the scan, but they didn't need to sedate Frank. He's already absolutely still. He's breathing, but that's all. He *is* breathing though. He is breathing. And Danny's there, holding his hand.

So I sit and look at the ground. Even the blue line on the floor directing you to x-ray has stopped. Nobody needs directing to CT scanning. It's like the morgue, the sort of place the public don't go. You get taken to CT on a trolley. Oh God.

Encephalitis. Meningitis. What else can it be? If I'd have brought Frankie to hospital last night they'd have given i.v. antibiotics and he might have had a chance. But it's got to be too late now.

He's probably been like this all night, whilst we thought he was just sleeping it off, leaving the bacteria and toxins free to eat away at his brain, damaging it. My lovely, super-sociable little boy with the dimpled-cheeked, Mabel Lucy Atwell smile, adored by everyone, the star of his nursery ('Hi Frankie,' the little girls all cry when he arrives, 'Bye Frankie', they chorus when he leaves, and the staff laugh indulgently: 'Oh he's a bit of a one, your Frank, so much energy, so much charm, and those dimples...') All gone, because I was too stupid, or proud, to seek help, when I knew we needed it.

I'll go mad if I sit here, I need to do something, so I buy a newspaper from the hospital shop. Not that I care in the slightest what's happening in the world, but I need change for the phone. No mobiles allowed in hospital.

"Dan can't come to work today, his son's in hospital ... Thank you ... I hope so too."

"Can you pick Art up from school? Frank's very poorly. You'll keep him overnight? And take him to school tomorrow? Oh, thanks, Katrina."

"Is that Priestville Infants? Frank's in hospital, so Katrina will collect Art. Er, yes, I think it probably is quite serious."

"Message for Di. It's Em Pike here, I can't make my ante-natal appointment, Frank's in hospital."

What else? I was supposed to be meeting Sam for coffee. Another answering machine. I managed to keep it together for a proper person, but not another answering machine. "Frank's poorly," I sob. "I think he's got encephalitis, I can't come for coffee."

Encephalitis. What else could it be? What else could it be that was treatable? An abscess? They could drain that. A bleed? They could drain a subdural haematoma and children often made remarkable recoveries from strokes. A brain tumour? I think I'd rather a brain tumour than encephalitis. At least there was something you could do about a tumour.

I remember a long ago lecture on childhood disability. The Consultant told we GP trainees about the dazzling, happy little Susan. The thrust of the lecture had been the wonderful, caring, stoic parents. Parents who took their little girl immediately to the GP. The GP had seen her and called a 999 ambulance without delay. Herpes encephalitis: the vicious sibling of innocent little cold sores and chicken pox, but still potentially treatable with antiviral medication. At the hospital, they filled Susan with aciclovir within hours, as fast as they possibly could. Nobody could have done any better for this little girl, nobody wasted a second in phoning the GP, or getting her into hospital, or treating her once she got there, but still Susan is severely damaged. She can't walk or talk. She bangs her head against the wall and she screams. Perhaps in pain, perhaps in frustration. No one really knows. Susan can't tell them. She doesn't even recognise her parents and, worst of all, there's no rest, for her, or for her family, as she doesn't sleep. She wakes every two hours and screams. Her parents care for her as lovingly as they did when she was their perfect, happy, clever little girl. I didn't even have children at the time, but still I remember wiping tears away, for Susan and her poor parents. Now I was weeping for Susan and her parents and Frank. And me.

I phone my Mum, four hours away. My Dad answers. I start to get a bit weepy. He hands me straight over to my Mum. I pull myself together and manage to sound calm.

"Of course we'll come. It sounds like you've got Art sorted tonight, so is it alright if we come tomorrow, in time to get Art from school? We've got people round tonight."

"Okay." I'd obviously sounded too calm.

We're back on the ward; the side ward opposite the nurses' station. The place where they put the really poorly ones. I stroke Frank's hand, still a podgy baby hand, all splinted up for the drip. Not that Frank notices. He didn't even notice them put the drip in, or take the blood tests, or place the arterial line in his wrist that took three attempts and needed the consultant to do in the end. The CT scan is normal. Is that good? It must be good surely, if there's no swelling, or necrotic areas, or cancer. It also means there's not anything obviously treatable, no bleeds or abscesses to drain. Frank has an EEG next, multiple electrodes spread across his scalp, looking alien, horrible and painful, but only held on by suction and jelly. It only takes minutes, then they rub the jelly out of his hair. Frank hates having his hair washed or ruffled, but he doesn't move. The perfect patient, motionless on the bed. Crucified, almost, with an oxygen mask on his face, a pulse oximeter flashing its little red light through his finger, with a drip in one arm and an arterial line in the other and a little bag over his penis to catch a urine specimen so they can look for toxins and metabolites and anything else that might explain why he's like this. They've already sent a battery of blood tests to the lab. Serum rhubarbs, they were known as at medical school: those rare conditions that clever hospital doctors always like to test for but are so rare that no-one ever actually suffers from. Not that encephalitis is common. Very uncommon. In fact, I've never seen it. Not even in Africa. I have seen the after-effects though. Like little Susan, not that I ever met Susan. Meningitis is a lot more common, but still pretty rare. I've seen maybe ten cases of that in sixteen years as a doctor. But they're filling Frank up with antibiotics to cover meningitis, and of course the aciclovir for herpes encephalitis, although aciclovir never did little Susan any good.

I don't want to leave his side, but I've got to go for a pee. Frank's notes are lying open at the nursing station and I sneak a look. His blood count has dropped to only 7.9 (stress reaction I suppose, but quite a drop), white cell count is 60 (Dr. Jones had said it was high, but not that high!), his C.R.P. is 549 (again Dr. Jones said it was up, but God, I didn't even know it could go that high). So it's definitely infection, and there doesn't seem to be anywhere else it can be other than in his head. The EEG is grossly deranged: 'changes consistent with encephalitis', they said. So that's it, then. Encephalitis. Unless he's had some sort of poisoning or overdose. Dr. Jones asks us if that's possible? Could Frankie have taken something from the cupboard or my medical bag? God, could he? Anything's possible. The house is such a mess and I'm not as careful as I should be. Guilt.

Danny goes home to check the cupboards and medicine cabinet. We consider phoning Danny's parents, but Danny says no. Who would that help? Peg and Bob adore their little grandsons, but Peg in particular is such a worrier, and distraught over Mick being still unable to swallow and losing weight. She thinks Mick's got cancer, Mick thinks he's got cancer and I think Mick's got cancer, so it's hard to be at all reassuring to either Mick or his Mum or Dad. We can't tell them about Frankie. There's still no word of Mick's appointment. Shit. I was supposed to be chasing it up, using what little influence I had as a doctor to get something done. I phone Mick directly, who sounded like he was having difficulty with fluids now.

"Had you told Dr. F you're struggling with a cup of tea?"

"Yes. Last week."

"Well tell him again. No, don't bother, just blooming well turn up to casualty and refuse to leave. I'm serious, Mick, you need it sorted."

Mick coughs. "But last time I went, they said I just had a sore throat."

"That was ages ago – now you're choking on your tea. Go today. Now."

I don't have the time or energy to mess around with the proper channels. I don't mention Frank, in fact for a minute there, I'd forgotten about him. Oh Frankie!

I need to talk to someone. A medical person who will understand what I mean by 'encephalitis' and a 'w.c.c. count of 60' and a 'grossly disturbed EEG', and who won't say things like 'I'm sure Frank will be fine', when quite clearly Frankie is very unlikely to be fine. I phone my non PC, totally non-touchy-feely GP partner to tell him what was happening. Charles doesn't make any inappropriate soothing noises. He just asks me some factual questions:

"Has Frank had a lumbar puncture?"

"No. They say he's too poorly and on all the antibiotics anyway. They might do it tomorrow."

"Was his C.R.P. really 549? I've never seen one more than 300. Wouldn't you expect some changes on the CT if you had encephalitis?"

"Apparently there's often nothing to see at first. Unless it's really bad."

"Okay, well, that's something. Look, you'll have to get some sleep. If Danny's staying at the hospital tonight, you can't go home to an empty house. Come and stay with us. Either Ruth or I can drive you back in if there's any change for the worse. Or if you go into labour."

Oh God, I'd forgotten. I'm supposed to be having a baby.

Frank has torrential black diarrhoea, all over the bed. Malaena. A stress bleed probably. His body is packing in. We turn him and clean him, then I hold him whilst the nurses strip the bed. They are lovely, the nurses. Just do what needs to be done. They ask me if I'm okay holding him standing up (the drip tubing isn't long enough for me to sit down), in 'my condition'. Yes, I say. This is the first time I've had the chance to hold him. Frank's a solid little fellow, and even heavier with his limbs and head flopping. I hope that being in his mother's arms may stimulate a response of some sort ... but nothing. They put him into a big nappy. That upsets me. We finished potty training months ago. I remain calm though, as I've remained calm all day, apart from Sam's answering machine, sort of floating above it. Denial, I think they call it.

Danny's back with a tape recorder and music and Grey Bear and sandwiches and books. He kisses me and asks if there's any change. "No," I say. There's nothing else to say. I wanted to have made Frank miraculously better for his Dad, just by my presence, or sheer force of will, but he's still lying stiller than I ever thought possible for a child, especially my hyperactive one. But strangely peaceful. They put the night light on and I leave. I don't kiss Frank goodbye. I don't kiss Danny goodbye. I just leave.

Art would be in bed at Katrina's by now, so I go straight to Charles and Ruth's. They're great. I have a shower and they feed me supper and a glass of wine. I've had nothing to eat all day and find I am hungry. The wine works wonders and I relax enough to tease Charles about not pouring himself another in case he needs to drive me to Delivery Ward. Denial, I think it's called. We laugh about the time when Charles visited me and baby Art on the post-natal ward during 'partners only' visiting. The staff looked a little embarrassed when Charles said he was my partner and whispered that they thought my husband was already with me. What would they say this time, if Charles has to drive me in, in labour?

We laugh again, a shared response to bond the group when the danger has passed. But the danger hasn't passed.

Charles and Ruth say goodnight. I know I'm lucky to have such good friends, but I don't want to go to bed and be alone. I wonder about phoning the ward, but I'm too scared. I'm an optimist, so at least I can hope. I don't want to be told that my hopes are false. I don't want to hear that he's worse, so I don't ring. I just spend the night wondering about phoning. Wondering how Frankie is. Wishing I was there. Thinking I should be there, glad not to be there, just watching Frankie lying, but unable to do anything to make it better.

I wonder if I could cope with a child as disabled as Susan. I'm sure I could not. I think I would rather Frankie died. This is awful, I can't wish that. I will be able to cope with disability, I'm sure we'll manage. At least I have Danny, so much more patient than I. I'll just keep thinking of what I once had and lost by my own neglect. I don't think I could bear it. Physical disability I could cope with, and perhaps some mental damage. Just some mental damage. Learning disability they call it. And there's a spectrum, mild, medium, and severe. I couldn't cope with the severe. What was my cut-off? Oh God, I wasn't sure. This was awful. I certainly had a cut-off, I knew that – not like Susan's parents. Not talking? Would I prefer my son to die just because he couldn't talk? Surely not? Possibly. It would be okay if he could smile, I think. That was my cut-off for what made life worth living. To be able to smile. Certainly for Frank. He had such a lovely smile. God, please let him still be able to smile. Whatever it takes, I'll do anything. Finally exhaustion takes over and I doze for a couple of hours.

I have breakfast with Charles and Ruth with their two, healthy kids laughing, arguing and shouting. The kind of breakfast Danny and I used to call stressful: all that noise so early in the morning when we all had to be out. Today I'm jealous of all this normality. Soon all is quiet again, alone in my car, only able to think that Frank's unconscious and it's all my fault. Every day he stays unconscious, the prognosis will be worse. The white cell count of 60, the C.R.P. of over 500, all that infection, all in his brain. But he'll have had 24 hours of treatment now, so there should be some sign of recovery – if there's going to be any recovery. Yesterday, I must have believed he was going to get better really, otherwise why so calm? Today was the crunch. Today would determine if we were going to get Frank back, back smiling at least. Suddenly I feel panicky and cold. The creeping dread of bad news, really bad news. I'd never really experienced it before, not on my own behalf. There's been Granny and Ahcong dying, but they came to a natural end to good, full lives. Not Frank, he's only just turned three. I sit at the traffic lights sobbing. I miss the change to green and someone toots. Rush hour. People had places to go. Important lives to lead, they couldn't miss twenty seconds at a traffic light. Yesterday, I would have pounded the horn at someone daydreaming at green.

Frankie's no worse. No better.

"Frank's remained a good colour and his temperature's down. His pupils have never been dilated and we haven't needed to ventilate him, which is good. His oxygen saturation has never dipped below 97 percent. The good news is that he hasn't had convulsions. Obviously if he does get any worse we'll have to transfer him to ITU."

The best Dr. Jones was saying to us was that Frankie wasn't actually brain dead. No. No. I had to stay optimistic. Despair helps no-one. Dr. Jones was giving good news. Frankie wasn't damaged enough to have fits. He'd never stopped breathing, so his brain wouldn't be damaged further by lack of oxygen. And Frank actually looked well. Even though he wasn't moving, he looked well. Very still, very peaceful. Like a nice, long sleep. I feel a real surge of hope.

"What's his prognosis from here?" I ask, eagerly looking for the upbeat, optimistic answer we doctors always try to find for our patients, if at all possible.

"Well...we have seen some children make some progress from this point..."

"Oh." Not the answer I was looking for. Danny squeezed my shoulder. Danny's been up all night and he looks exhausted. I send him home for some sleep.

The dayshift was probably a lot easier – lots of visitors and things going on to take my mind off the thought of Frank never smiling again. They do the chest x-ray they'd talked about yesterday, just as a routine, and the lumbar puncture that he was too unstable to do yesterday. They send me away for the lumbar puncture, but I have nowhere to go. I buy another newspaper that I won't read. Apart from the date. October 1st. D Day. Sorry baby. Please stay in there for a while, until Frankie's better. Oh God, I'm assuming he's going to get better. I try to pray, but I don't really know how. Please make Frankie better. I'll do...anything.

Nothing on the lumbar puncture.

"Good news?" I ask eagerly.

"Well, encephalitis probably wouldn't show up anyway."

My GP comes to see me, takes one look at Frankie and gives me a hug. There's nothing else Ana can do but it helps. Di comes to give me my ante-natal check, all laughing as she enters, until she sees Frank stretched out.

"Oh, Em, I'm sorry. I hadn't realized ... I thought he'd maybe just broken his arm or something."

I tell Di I won't be having a home birth. I'll probably still be in hospital with Frank and even if I'm not I'm not going to be in the right frame of mind. Di promises to deliver my new baby herself, in or out of hospital, and do whatever she can. I feel a bit better. Di hugs me too and leaves. I know some lovely people. I realise that I am a very lucky person. We both forget to have any ante-natal checks. Then Charles pops in between surgeries, just as Dr. Jones arrives clutching an x-ray. Charles holds out his hand.

"Charles Gale. Em's partner."

"Er, right." Dr. Jones looks round for Danny with a little confused frown. "Er, I've got something to show you. Do you want, um Mr. er...?"

"Dr. Charles Gale, Em's partner at West Hill Surgery."

"Ah, yes. Sorry. I thought you looked familiar."

"...and yes, I'd like Charles to stay."

Dr. Jones produced a chest x-ray.

"Frankie's got pneumonia!!!" I squeal with delight. "Frankie's got pneumonia. It's just pneumonia!"

Pneumonia. All those infectious markers, because he has pneumonia. Pneumonia's curable. He's on all the right antibiotics. Bloody hell, it's just pneumonia!

"It's certainly a pretty impressive white-out," says Charles. "His whole middle lobe. This is good news, isn't it?"

"Well, probably. It gives a reason for the infection, but Frank's still unconscious, we're not quite sure why. It may be toxins giving an encephalopathy, which would hopefully be reversible, and may not leave too much lasting damage, but he has been unconscious for thirty-six hours now..."

I wasn't really listening to the last bit. Frank has pneumonia and it was being treated. He'll be alright, I knew it. I was an optimist.

I rush to phone Danny.

"Frank's got pneumonia!"

"Has he? Are you alright? Why do you sound so pleased?"

"It's just pneumonia. They still don't really know why he's unconscious, but pneumonia is treatable and all that infection is in his lung and not in his brain."

Danny comes straight in. There's still no response. My surge of optimism has faded. Perhaps it was just pneumonia, but pneumonia is still a killer, and if it is a funny strain that can send toxins to the brain, well that's almost worse, because that really would have been curable if I'd brought Frank in the night before. Danny says I ought to go home now, to see Art - not quite five years old and completely forgotten about.

My parents have arrived. My mum is putting Art to bed and my Dad is doing the crossword. There's something soothing about all this normality. I am so very glad to see them. Art is having a great time, he had a night at Katrina's, then Grandma Kat to play with and no Frankie to compete with. He hasn't missed me at all.

I do manage some sleep this time. Pneumonia. It's still enough to give me hope.

Danny phones. Frank woke up and asked for a drink! Really? Really? I ask, and leap into the car without brushing my teeth or hair. But Frankie is still completely motionless by the time I get there. Not a flicker. And not a flicker the whole 14 hours I am there. I accuse Danny of lying, just to keep my spirits up.

"Frankie did ask for a drink. Honest. It was wonderful. I'm sorry you missed it, but he's there, Em. He's still there."

"Did he drink the drink when he got it?"

"Well...no. He went back to sleep."

"Did he smile?"

"What? No. The lad's poorly, he probably doesn't feel like smiling."

"I want him to smile, or even just open his eyes."

"He's going to be alright. You said so yourself. Pretty high functioning you said, to be able to ask for a drink."

"If he really did ask for a drink ..."

"Em, he asked for a drink."

"Talking. No smiling. No recognition. Most autistic children can talk. I don't want my child to be autistic and be unable to relate to me, or you. That's the worst thing."

Worry kills optimism.

The doctors on the ward round obviously didn't believe Danny either. Dr. Jones is off for the weekend, so it's Dr. Brown today. None of the nurses heard the alleged 'I need a drink' and there hadn't even been even the slightest of groans when they took blood from him.

"I'm Dr. Brown. How are you feeling, Frank?" Dr. Brown asks in that way that doctors do, especially in teaching the juniors mode, to show them they shouldn't just ask the mum how the child is, when the child can speak for themselves. And you should always speak to an unconscious child as though they can hear you, because sometimes they can. Of course no-one ever believes it really, apart from Robin Williams pretending to be a doctor in a schmaltzy film. You can be *too* optimistic. So Dr. Brown asks Frank how he's feeling. No reply. Nothing. No, one looked surprised.

"Have you any pain anywhere, Frank?" Nothing. Dr. Brown turns to discuss some point with the juniors, probably how you should always talk to an unconscious child as though they can hear you. Just then there was a slight movement from the bed. Frankie? A little hand lifts up ... stretches over ... and pats his opposite wrist, where the drip had tissued, leaving a sore, swollen spot.

Oh! Oh! Frankie. Oh! I start sobbing. This must be the best moment of my life. Dr. Brown laughs and his juniors laugh and the nurses wipe away tears. Danny and I do both. A real, unreal, Robin Williams moment. Back from the dead. Life triumphing over adversity. Great, great, great. Thank you, thank you, thank you.

Frank goes back to sleep, but he's alive, he's here, he can hear, he can understand. He's going to be better. He's not going to be autistic. He's going to smile.

I go home to sleep.

On my way out, I sneak another look at his notes. Blood count better at 9g, white count down to 30, still pretty high, but much better, and his biochemistry ... God! His potassium is 1.9! 1.9 – that's dangerously low. Frankie could have a cardiac arrest at that level. They can't let that happen, not today, not after that wonderful moment when he told us all his brain was alive and functioning. Dr. Brown has long gone, but I try and find the on call junior. I lie.

"Er, excuse me. They mentioned Frank's potassium was low. How low?"

The young doctor rifled through Frank's notes. "Okay, it was er ...1.9."

"But 1.9 is *really* low. Have you checked it again?"

"I'm a bit busy with new admissions. Other poorly children," the young doctor adds, pointedly.

"Yes, I know. But 1.9 is really *very* low."

"We're giving some potassium in the drip."

"But not very much."

"It's dangerous to give too much potassium..."

"And equally dangerous to give too little. Have you checked it again?"

"It's probably a lab artefact," the lad tries to reassure me, "We'll check it in the morning."

"Okay," I say, and drive home.

A mile down the road, it suddenly hits me. I'm being pathetic and passive again. 1.9 is bloody well NOT okay. I wouldn't dream of leaving a patient of mine with a potassium of 2.5, never mind under 2, never mind my own son. You can't leave it until morning. The young doctor's probably just a very junior junior, maybe he hasn't even told Dr. Brown. Maybe it *is* an artefact. Probably it's an artefact, but you can't just say that about every result you don't like. You've got HIV Mr. Mercury. Don't worry, it's probably just lab error. You weigh 12 and a half stones, Em. Nah, don't bother dieting, it's probably just an artefact.

Yes, they *had* added potassium to his drip, but Frankie had hardly actually had any, because they kept turning the drip off to put the intravenous antibiotics in.

I stop the car. They've got to check it tonight. My mobile's not charged. I never use the bloody thing. I drive on to the nearest phone box. I've got to be assertive. I ask to be put through to Children's Ward. I don't know the young doctor's name, but he's probably still sitting at the nursing station. It was only five minutes ago.

"It's Emily Pike here, I was just talking to you about Frank." I sob into the phone. "I know I sound like a pushy doctor parent but *please* check his potassium. Please." So much for being assertive. "I'm sorry. Yes it might be an artefact, but Frank responded today, it would be awful if he arrested now, for the sake of a bit of potassium. Please check it. Now."

"I'll ring you later with the result. Okay?"

"Thank you," I squeak in a little voice. "Thank you."

The phone rings while I am brushing my teeth. "3.1" Still low, but better. It was an artefact. I go to bed.

Danny rings at seven. Frankie's awake! He's talking and laughing and drawing pictures!

In my excitement, I nearly crash on the way into the hospital, but by the time I arrive Frank's sound asleep again. Six hours later though, he just wouldn't shut up. Talk, talk, talk, talk, talk. It was as if his speech had jumped to a higher plane whilst he was asleep, learning a whole new vocabulary. Perhaps his brain had just needed a rest so it could piece together the language puzzle. I told you sleep was important! Wonderful. We decide it's safe to tell Danny's parents that Frank's in hospital.

"...Frank's had pneumonia. Yes, fine now, though. Hopefully he'll be out tomorrow. No, no. He's absolutely fine." Peg and Bob were upset to hear that Frank had been poorly, and relieved he was better, but they couldn't share our happiness, not having known how Frankie had been, not while Mick was so ill.

Frankie's whizzing up and down the hospital corridor in the Cozy Coupe whilst I'm on phone. I really didn't want to think about poor Mick, but I had to ask. "How's Mick? Did he go to casualty? To his GP? Okay. What did he say? The appointment was coming. Right. Has it come? No. Okay, why don't you ring appointments direct? Meanwhile if it gets any worse ..."

Frankie nearly knocks over Dr. Jones, back for the Monday morning ward round. Dr. Jones smiles at Frankie, without any sign of recognition and I see him walk into Frank's room. Seconds later Dr. Jones reappears.

"Where's Frank?" The nurse laughs and points at the dangerous driver, smiling his cheeky dimpled smile from behind the wheel and heading back down the corridor.

"What? *That's* Frankie?!! I don't believe it!"

Our miracle boy, risen from the dead. Life triumphs over adversity once more. Dr. Jones is so impressed he says we can go home in the morning. I will be eternally grateful for my beautiful children and the gift of life. I will never allow worry to kill optimism and I will never complain about anything, ever again.

14. Life Won't Wait.

"A baby is God's opinion that life should go on." Carl
Sanburg, American Poet (1878-1967)

Hello? Anybody out there? It's me. Baby Pike III. Anybody
remember me? I've been trying to kick, but Mummy hasn't even
noticed. The one good thing about Frank being poorly, other
than him getting better, of course, is that Mummy genuinely
doesn't care if I'm a boy or a girl any more. So the pressure's off.
She's in a rotten old mood tonight, though. It was very late by the
time they let us out of the hospital. We had to wait for that nice
Dr. Jones, then we had to wait ages for Frankie's tablets, then it
was so late we all got stuck in the rush hour traffic. We're back
home now and the house is *so* noisy. Grandma Kat, Grandpa
John, Grandpa Bob and Grandma Peg are all here to see Frankie
and 'The Dogs' are making that funny, loud, coughing sort of
noise that they make and the phone keeps ringing and now
Art's 'throwing a massive tantrum'. Mummy says it's because he's
had the undivided attention of all his grandparents all day and
isn't pleased that everyone just wants to see Frankie. Oh no,
now Frankie's started screaming too. I don't remember Frankie
doing that tantrum thing before, but Mummy says it's because
he's tired and 'overstimulated'. Grandma Kat made a big dinner
for everyone, but because we're so late back from the hospital
Grandma Peg and Grandpa Bob just want to go home to Uncle
Mick, and are saying they only really want a sausage sandwich
anyway. Daddy is saying he doesn't have time for dinner as he
has to go to his 'rehearsal' as he'd missed three and the play is
next week. Mummy isn't very pleased with Daddy and Daddy
isn't very pleased with Mummy as they'd already talked about

it and she said he could go as long as I wasn't actually going to be born. She's saying she didn't and Daddy's saying she did (she did, but no-one's asking me) so Daddy goes anyway and Frankie starts screaming again, then Art starts screaming and Mummy starts crying and Grandma Kat's making noises in the kitchen making her dinner that no-one is eating, saying nothing at all. And Mummy said this was the best day of her life this morning! Hmmph. I've had enough of this. I'm going to sleep.

Good morning! It's a new day and everybody is happy again, thank goodness. We're out for 'walkies' with Grandpa John and 'The Dogs'. Grandma Kat has taken Art to school then is going to 'Tescos' with Frankie (who just won't stop talking) and Daddy has gone back to work saying he really ought to put in an appearance. Hoi, I thought I was the one due to be making the appearance!

Today's the day, my time has finally come. I know it. The first of October has been and gone, and I can't stay standing on my head until 1st of November just for the sake of family tradition. Mummy's prostaglandins are flowing and I'm squeezed down so tight into Mummy's pelvis that I can't breathe. Not that I can actually breathe, but we babies like to have some practice movements so we can give full throttle for the big entry. Mummy's supposed to be doing nice relaxing deep breaths too, like she advises her patients, but I don't remember her ever doing any of that. Hypocrite. It's all rush, rush, rush with her. Like now. I usually quite enjoy 'walkies'. It's nice and bouncy and sends the blood whooshing in and out of my umbilical cord, giving me a good clear out. But I'm not so sure today: 'walkies' is bouncing my head even deeper into her pelvis, and the walls of my home are tightening round me, like an overenthusiastic total body cuddle. Hmmm? I'm not sure I like it, but it only lasts a minute. Mummy's feeling it too, but is busy pretending she doesn't. We slow down a bit and she stops talking to Grandpa John until it's gone, then she starts again. "It's a lovely day," she's saying. She slows again. Another tightening. Must say that one was rather more than a cuddle, but there have been a few of these before.

Braxton Hicks contractions, Mummy calls them. A very grand name for a big squeeze.

Oooh, Mummy! We stop. That one almost took my practice breath away.

"I think we'd better go home, Dad. Something's happening."

I think you better had, Mummy. Something certainly is, and I don't know about you, but I'm feeling a little anxious. Well, I suppose now is a good a time as any. Life won't wait. Oooooooof!

Mummy phones Daddy.

"...right now?" Daddy's asking. "I was going to try and see Mick in my lunch hour"

"Well..."

Now, Mummy, NOW. Never mind Uncle Mick. Ooooooof.

"Now! Please."

Oh, oh, where's my bath gone? It's all draining away. Why's it all draining away? Ooooof! The walls are crushing me. Did I say I wanted to come out? Mummy's telling Daddy there's no time for a cup of tea and Grandma Kat is getting some towels so my dirty bathwater doesn't get all over the car seats. No, no, it's okay, Daddy, have your cup of tea, I'll stay inside. The first of November is fine by me. I'VE CHANGED MY MIND!

We're at the hospital and that nice midwife Di is waiting for us. Thank goodness Mummy gave up that daft idea of having me at home. Di promised to deliver me, even in the hospital and here she is, so I feel a bit better about it all ... well, until the next contraction. Ooof! I've resigned myself to fate. Mummy's a big strong girl with a nice wide pelvis, and she's done it before, so there's no reason for any problems. Di knows what she is doing. Oooooof.

"Try to slow your breathing down," Di says. Okay Di, I'll slow my practice breathing. "Well, Em, you're four centimetres dilated."

IS THAT ALL?!! Less than half way? You must be kidding! Mummy just groans in disappointment. It's only been a few hours since we were out walking, but Mummy's had a bad week and I'm not sure she's up for much more of this. Neither am I, let me tell you, and I am a Pike baby, so that makes me very competitive and determined. So if you'll excuse me, that's Mummy getting into the birthing pool*, so I'm going to have to stop talking and concentrate. Short, sharp, round that bend and out. Don't cry Mummy, I'm coming, I'm coming.

What's this, who's patting my head? I'm in a bath again. Okay. That's fine, I liked my bath of amniotic fluid, and now my head is out of that clamp, I can talk again. Now if I could just get my chest out. Mummy gives a push and I swim out. Di's lifting me up and onto Mummy's tummy. Phew! I'm exhausted. I just lie there on a nice, warm, soft tummy. I've got no energy to cry. I open my eyes. Can't see much. So this is life, is it? I can just make out a blurry face, crying and crying and crying. Is that you Mummy? Hello? Aren't you supposed to be pleased? I blink. Is that a smile? I haven't seen a smile before. I think she's smiling. Yes. That's okay, then. That's right, she did cry when Frank said his drip site hurt, so I think this must be what they call 'tears of joy'. I've got my head on her chest now and there's an arm round me. I can still hear her heartbeat, although it's not as loud as it was inside. There's another blurry face. That one's definitely smiling, laughing even. Daddy? He's stroking my head. Ooh! What was that? Di's just cut my cord. I'm here, I'm here. Hello everybody. Hello! Oh, by the way. What am I? Girl or boy? No-one's asked yet. Mummy's holding me round the bottom, so Di can't see. Ach, who cares?

Mummy had had enough of hospitals, so Di lets us home within two hours. Mummy put me into something called a nappy, then a 'baby-gro', then a 'car seat' – none of which I am particularly impressed with, preferring my nice warm bath of amniotic fluid. Still. I'm here, I don't have to go through that 'being born' thing ever again and I'm healthy, so mustn't grumble. Mummy sits in the back of the car next to me and phones Grandma Kat.

"Can you make some dinner, Mum, I'm starving!"

Grandpa John feeds Mummy some stuff called champagne, which is very nice, thank you, mixed in with that nice, thick, creamy, colustrum stuff that is just on tap from Mummy if I make a crying noise. Lots of blurry faces come and look at me, mostly looking a bit like Mummy. I think I have worked out which ones are Art and Frank – a bit smaller, a lot noisier and come much closer than the others, and then of course there are the two called Rogie and Bo, which are hairier and make a lot of sniffing noises and have wet things called tongues to clean my face. Yawn. I'm going to sleep. It's an exhausting business getting born.

Heart-stoppingly beautiful. That's what the lady called me. Three days old and I'm heart-stoppingly beautiful! I'd give her a smile, but I can't do it yet. I'm sitting in a car seat in the park with Grandma Kat whilst Mummy goes to the Registrar, to tell them I officially exist. Ella Margaret Pike. Female. 4th of October 2001.

Everyone is gratifyingly impressed with me. "She's beautiful" is the consensus, which I'm sure is a good thing, but today's heart-stoppingly beautiful I think is probably even better. The only problem is getting milk from Mummy. Her feeders have become so swollen that I can't get my mouth round them, and I'm getting very tired. This life business is terribly tiring – so much more noise and faces to see, and being lifted up and cuddled, and having my bottom wiped with cold cloths, then put in another 'nappy'. Can't she just fill that plastic bath with nice warm amniotic fluid and leave me there? I just want to sleep. Really, it's too tiring and difficult to suck those feeders and I'm getting too tired to bother. Got a bit of a headache too. Think I'll just sleep it off. Life is exhausting!

* Water Births:
A recent anecdotal report (on one case) in the BMJ suggests a water birth may have more risks that first realised. A stressed baby may inadvertently gasp once released from the grip of the birth canal and inhale birthing pool water.

Like all things there are pros and cons. There is, of course, nothing natural about a human giving birth in water. Nor is it natural to have an epidural or a caesarean section. If you reduce the mother's need for analgesia you will reduce some risks, and create others.

15. Optimists Don't Worry

"There is no finer investment for any community than putting milk into babies." Winston Churchill

There was nothing specific, but I was getting worried. Ella had latched on beautifully that first day, but suddenly she seemed to have lost the knack. It was those big boobs of mine, swollen up to an unmanageable size again. Oh no, not another traumatic breastfeeding saga. Ella was sleeping a lot, nearly all the time. Great for the first couple of nights, but, well, she wasn't really feeding. Friends came and once again admired Ella's heart-stopping beauty, sleeping so peacefully. Why was I complaining? I spent the last five years complaining that the boys wouldn't sleep and now I had a sleeping beauty and I wasn't happy.

Ella woke up crying, but it was a funny cry, more of mewl, like a distressed kitten. That wasn't right, that sounded like the high-pitched cry of meningitis. Honestly, doctor mothers are the worst! Optimists don't worry. Em, pull yourself together, you're just being paranoid, because of Frank. Ella looks fine, doesn't she? Not hot, nice peaceful breathing, no rash, not floppy or anything, just sleepy. I was just having a bit of a problem feeding her, which wasn't at all unusual and Ana had checked her over and like everyone else she said that Ella was just perfect.

Ana had been lovely, just like she was when she came to see me in hospital with Frank. Pity about her receptionist.

"You left hospital before the doctor could do the baby's newborn check," accused the receptionist.

"Er, yes. Di checked her over and she was fine, and said the GP would come and do it today."

"Very well. Can you pop up to the surgery this afternoon?"

What? Ella was fifteen hours old and Danny had just gone back to work.

"Er, well ..." Have you had children? I wanted to shout down the phone. In your day, nobody got out of bed for the first ten days, never mind jumped in the car, drove across town, tried to get parked then carried a newborn in a car seat into a crowded surgery before they were even a day old. And, not wanting to be too terribly pathetic about all this, I think I had had an unusually stressful week. Charles and I visited all my new mums in our practice in the first week. Was it so much to ask that someone visited me? Of course I never said any of this. "Er. Can't the doctor come here?"

"They're all terribly busy today."

"Never mind. Di said she'd pop in and Ella's fine. I don't really need a doctor anyway."

But I was glad Ana came anyway. She told me about the newborn baby that survived ten days in the rubble in the Mexican Earthquake, and we both agreed Mother Nature made sure babies had plenty of stores until we got going with breastfeeding.

But that was two days ago and now Ella had a funny cry. I didn't care if I was being paranoid – I called the midwife. It was Vikki today. Vikki told me breastfed babies only take an average of 17 mls in the first day and 36ml on the second day etc., and that when we bottle fed them, it was effectively force feeding, as their poor little stomachs weren't designed for such big amounts at first. Vikki's facts and figures agreed totally with *Breast is Best* (long since eaten by worms, but I remembered it verbatim), and they were actually quite comforting. But what about that funny cry? I didn't like that cry. Vikki agreed with my own suggestion that I was just being over-anxious. Ella looked fine. And so she did, sleeping so peacefully. But Frank had slept peacefully too, for three days. And he looked fine too. Stop, Em. You are not a worrier by nature. What's got into you? Children. That's what. They turn the most sensible of women into jibbering wrecks.

But then a couple of hours later, I heard that funny little cry again, from the pram. That horrible mewl. No, it wasn't right. I didn't like it. And Ella just seemed too weak to take the breast.

Vikki had gone and Danny was out, so I took action, risking the wrath of the military wing of the Breast is Best Brigade. I sterilised a bottle and fed her. I didn't care if Vikki said it was force-feeding. Perhaps Ella was just weak with hunger, the poor little mite. She sucked the bottle a little tentatively at first, then glugged it down. I stroked Ella's fontanelle. It was soft and normal feeling, not bulging. No baby with meningitis would feed so well, not even from a bottle. I was being paranoid. I burped her and we smiled at each other (I'm sure she did, and I'm sure she said, 'thanks mum' too). Food – that's all she wanted. Bottom rung. A baby doesn't ask for much, really.

I put Ella in her car seat and she looked around. A healthy, alert baby. Frank was blowing raspberries right in her face and she was gazing right at him. See you silly woman, two perfectly healthy children, your imagination is just playing tricks. With this scene of domestic bliss and a full hour to go before Art came back from school, I made myself a cup of tea.

The phone rang. It was Danny.

"Mick went to Casualty last night and they admitted him directly."

"Thank goodness."

"Yes, but they couldn't do the endoscopy today because Mick 'didn't co-operate' with the tube."

"I'm not surprised." Poor Mick couldn't even swallow his tea, never mind a three foot long stiff hosepipe-cum-telescope. How was he ever going to 'co-operate'? "So what's their plan now?"

"A barium swallow," sighed Danny. "To think Mick waited all this time for the endoscopy suite to open, and they couldn't even do the endoscopy. Anyway, it's tomorrow."

Tomorrow came and went and Mick choked on the gloopy, chalky barium too. They decided to try another endoscopy, but put him to sleep this time.

Bob phoned this time, his voice bursting with relief. "It's not cancer. They say Mick's just got a pharyngeal pouch."

"Really?" I didn't mean to sound quite so surprised. "That's great, Bob. Pretty unusual, but it's just a little operation and it's sorted. That's really great."

"Yes, we're so pleased. And Peg's finally got a date for her knee replacement too."

"About time. Well that's just great, Bob."

Gosh. What surprisingly good news! This was the third time in a week that I had feared the worst. Enough pessimism, I was going to go back to expecting the best, it's just so much less traumatic. I felt fleetingly guilty that I'd used up my prayers for Frank and Ella, so hadn't really put in a proper request for Mick, but the prayers I would have made had been answered.

For 24 hours, everything was fine. Art was happy at school, Frankie was back at playgroup and I had a beautiful baby girl. If only I could breastfeed. *Breast is Best* was right. After the bottle Ella wasn't interested in the breast at all. I wrestled with her to latch her on, then a boy fell over, so I abandoned ship and put a plaster on the bleeding knee. I plonked the boys in front of a *Thunderbirds* video and tried again. Ella finally got a grip when I realised I hadn't shut the door properly and Bo was rooting through the nappy bin. I threw Bo out, washed my hands and tried again. Then the phone rang.

It was Danny. Mick's results were back. He had cancer, after all. Oh. Poor Mick. Of course he did. He was always going to. The pharyngeal thing was just a cruel false ray of hope. If they'd have told him that when he first went in, he would have been quite ready for it, but not after reassuring him it was just a rare benign condition then turning round and saying, no. sorry Sir, it's malignant after all. What's the answer, believe the best and be disappointed or believe the worst and be worried unnecessarily? Life is cruel, life is unfair, shit will happen. There's no point being surprised when it does, but there's no point worrying about it either. You need the facts first, so you can realistically assess them, accept them and move on. They hadn't waited for the facts on Mick, in fact we still hadn't got the full facts.

Peg was distraught and had cancelled her knee operation. Mick was apparently taking it very well, resigning himself to going for a scan the next day to see how far it had spread. Damn. Ella had lost her grip. I was going to have to start all over again to get her latched back on. Bugger. All this messing about was making my breasts SO sore. Within seconds I'd forgotten all about Mick. That was the trouble with breastfeeding. It made you very selfish, you couldn't think about anyone or anything other than getting your baby fed.

The most important thing in life must be food. And when you have a baby, the most important thing is feeding your baby. Worrying about Mick wasn't going to help him anyway. Or perhaps I was just making excuses.

I lined up mouth, nipple, gritted my teeth and plugged Ella in. She started sucking. I winced. It would ease off in a minute. Think cow, think cow. Then the phone rang again.

16. Dr. Jones' Double-Glazing

"We have discovered the secret to life..." Francis Crick 1956
on discovering the double helix structure of DNA with
James Watson (and a lot of help from Rosalind Franklin)

"Life is a system with inheritable genetic material..." various
biology teachers

"Can I speak to Dr. Pike?" This innocent question is guaranteed
to turn me from cheery optimist to stroppy cow. Well Danny
would disagree about the cheery optimist bit, and as has probably
become clear by now, right at that moment, I was at my least
loving and least forgiving and least optimistic: baby blues, bad
temper, cumulative insomnia, emotional exhaustion five days after
having a baby, a week after my three year old was unconscious in
hospital, with my brother-in-law terminally ill, my in-laws beside
themselves and my parents in an exhausted heap after the traumas
of the last week. All the elation of Frank's miraculous return to life
and my being granted a beautiful healthy girl had well and truly
worn off (oh, how quickly we forget to be grateful. Sorry, I've
said that before, but it's worth repeating).

If people must assign me a title, I am Dr. Joy or (at a push)
Mrs. Pike. The only people to call me Dr. Pike are double-glazing
salesman. Dr. Pike is actually worse than the totally random "Can
I speak to the homeowner?" because they've got little bits of
information about you, a bit like a stalker. Either way, I don't
want double-glazing, time share, amazing offers, special holidays,
BT customer survey, courtesy calls from Kwik Fit and certainly
not cold calls from politicians wanting my vote. So just in case
anyone is thinking of phoning me, I'm Dr. Joy at work and Mrs.

Pike at the school gate. You could call me half a feminist: one who grudgingly agreed to my husband's name as I'm proud to be the mother of my children (as long as they aren't having a tantrum or losing slugs in the supermarket) and also proud (90 percent of the time) to be wife to my husband. Being Mrs. Pike also offers a bit of anonymity from certain of my patients who rightly or wrongly feel that that awful, mean Dr. Joy owes them something. Most of my patients think I'm marvellous, of course (or at least, as an optimist/deluded egomaniac, I shall continue to labour under this illusion) but there are always one or two who fail to be won over by my charms. The patient who was so appalled that I was pregnant that he suggested I gave my baby up to a German adoption agency, for instance, or a few of my drug addicts whom I might have refused a prescription or a sick note for missing their community service three weeks ago. I don't want the aforesaid drug addict, now poverty-stricken with no methadone to sell, looking me up in the address book and making me pay for my generosity deficit with the family jewels. Although if it was family jewels he was after, he would be sorely disappointed – which would of course be worse, because then he could take his frustration out in acts of wanton violence or vandalism. Does this sound a bit too paranoid for an optimist?

These people who have no idea who you are (but would like your money anyway) always phone at teatime/bathtime/when you're on the toilet/the kids are screaming/fighting/vomiting or when the dinner is burning. Usually I just hang up, or snap back with a curt 'who are you?' or some such unfriendly greeting. I am rarely rude to anyone (well apart from Danny of course), and I do know, deep down that it's just some youngster trying to make a few quid to go to college, or a mum returning tentatively to the workplace years after having children, or some other poor bastard who's just doing their job for a pittance.

A good salesman will sell you all you never knew that you needed e.g.: did you know double-glazing was right up there on Maslow's hierarchy? A shelter and safety need. Or was it a self-esteem and status need? Or an aesthetic need?

"Um. Dr. Pike?" This voice on the phone sounded a little too tentative for a salesman, so I didn't hang up immediately, and it would have been difficult anyway, with Ella attached to the contralateral boob.

"Who's that?"

"Er, am I speaking to Dr. Pike?"

"Why?" I snapped. "What do you want?"

"Um, this is Dr. Jones."

"Oh." I probably did want to speak to Frank's Consultant. After all, Dr. Jones only knew that Frank Pike's mother was a doctor, so Dr. Pike was not a totally unreasonable assumption. "Sorry. I thought you were trying to sell me double glazing."

"Huh? Is this, er, a bad time, Dr. Pike?"

"No, no. It's as good a time as I'm ever going to get just now. It's just that most people that call me Dr. Pike or Mrs. Joy are trying to sell windows or time shares ... oh, never mind. Sorry. Frank's absolutely fine, whizzing around the back yard on his bike as we speak. Thank you all so much."

"Good. I was er, phoning with some news about Frank. We've got some results."

"Oh? He's great, absolutely fine." I didn't really care what Frank's results were. Some fascinating bug that caused a coma 1 in 10,000 cases perhaps, but it didn't matter what now, as obviously the cocktail of antibiotics had killed it off and Frankie was fine. "What results?"

"It looks as though Frank's got a metabolic abnormality of his fatty acid metabolism. Either MCAD or LCAD, we'll need to check more specialist results. That's long or medium chain acetyl co-A dehydrogenase deficiency..."

A metabolic disorder of fatty acid metabolism? One of those unforgiving genetic diseases that I had been so scared that Art might have when he was poorly with that big liver, which were invariably progressive, where you started out with a perfectly normal child who was unable to process some component of an ordinary diet so gradually they built up toxins that destroyed the neurological system and you ended up with a child first just behaving a bit peculiarly then unable to talk, or walk, and God!

I didn't know too much about the individual ones as there were thousands and all incredibly rare, but all I remembered from medical school is that most were pretty ghastly. Like Lorenzo, in the film *Lorenzo's Oil*, where the totally devoted parents nursed their horribly damaged son, who had been such a bright, loving intelligent boy, just like Frankie, refusing to give up on him against all the odds, and discovering a combination of oils that might help reverse the progress. But their oils were all too late for Lorenzo, although it did help some other children who were diagnosed earlier, delaying some of the damage, but it was all too horrible to contemplate for any child, and certainly not for *my* child. Life is cruel. Life is so, so cruel. And it was genetic so there was a chance that the other children would be affected too. GOD, NO! I watched Frankie, my adorable, cheeky chappy do a hand-brake turn round the fir tree on his red fire brigade bike, getting a few twigs tangled in the stabilisers. "But Frankie's absolutely fine!"

"Yes, and we'll need to double-check the tests. Do you know about the disorders of fatty acid metabolism? They're very rare."

"Well, no, not much." I felt the same cold dread that had crept over me when we couldn't wake Frankie up, and again when he was stretched out in paediatric resus, surrounded by doctors and nurses and tubes. Without knowing any of the details, none of these metabolic disorders were good news. Lorenzo had one faulty gene. Out of 50,000. When we already share over 99 percent of our genetic makeup with each other, and 98 percent with the apes, how come just one gene that's a little bit different can cause so much damage?

"It seems that Frank can't metabolise his fatty acids into ketones when he's under stress, so when he runs out of his glucose and glycogen stores, he metabolises them by different pathways, which can cause toxins, which causes encephalopathy, which is why he was unconscious."

"But FRANKIE'S FINE."

"Yes, as it happened we gave him glucose solution anyway. Of course, if we'd known he had MCAD, we'd have given him a stronger solution and he might have come round quicker, but it's very rare. It means if he's ever ill, you'll need to give him glucose, and if he won't take an oral solution he'll need to be admitted for a glucose drip."

"And long term, what's the damage?"

"Well, there isn't usually too much of a problem, as long as he gets his glucose."

"You mean it's not progressive? Not like Lorenzo?"

"Lorenzo?"

"*Lorenzo's Oil*. I can't remember the full name."

"You mean Adrenoleucodystrophy? Yes, I see what you're thinking. Another faulty gene for metabolising very long chain fatty acids. No. Not as long as Frank gets his glucose. You'll need to come in to get the other children tested, and some more specific tests for Frank. It's a recessive gene, which means a one in four chance for each child to get it, as you know of course."

"So it's not progressive? Not like Lorenzo?"

"Yes. I'm sorry to bring you this ..."

"...and it doesn't go on to cause brain damage?"

"No, not if Frank gets his glucose. Shall we say tomorrow on the ward?"

"So. Frank just needs a bit of glucose if he's poorly?"

"Yes. We'll see you tomorrow?"

"Is that all? Fine. Tomorrow. No problem."

No. No problem at all, just a bit of glucose. That's all. YES!!!

"Dr. Joy." Dr. Jones was learning. It was a week later.

"I'm afraid I've got some bad news."

"Oh?"

"I've got the results for the children and I'm afraid they all have MCAD. That's really very unlucky. With a recessive gene there's a one in 64 chance that all three of them have it."

"Oh. Okay. Is that all?"

"Is that all...?" Dr. Jones sounded a bit bemused.

"Well, I just have to feed them a bit of glucose if they're poorly, and worst case is that they have to be admitted for a glucose drip?"

"Er, yes."

"And there's nothing else you're not telling me. If we do that, it's not progressive?"

"Er. No. You did read the handout I gave you?"

Yes I did, and numerous internet sites and books to boot. MCAD* has a 25 percent mortality rate and 70 percent chance of some degree of brain damage, usually during an 'episode' like Frank's. Before it was discovered in the 1980s, they think it may have been a cause of cot death. You have a baby that sleeps through the night (you see, I never did, so for all I moaned and groaned, it probably saved their lives), then perhaps a little cold, or snuffly nose, so he doesn't really have a full feed before he goes to sleep, extending his overnight fast and he just doesn't wake up – just like Frank. Looking back this would explain Art's funny floppy do with his big liver at one year old, and Ella's strange mewling cry (God, her brain was probably becoming flooded with toxins too, just like Frank, and I was busy committing exactly the same error as I had with Frank – knowing something was wrong, not knowing what, and therefore doing nothing about it). Fortunately Art stopped vomiting and Ella took a bottle, but it was chilling reading about these poor, poor families with one, two or even three cot deaths, before they had ever even discovered MCAD existed, when just a little bit of glucose could have saved their children. Frank was in hospital around the time of the Sally Clarke appeal, then the Tripte Patel case (and subsequently others) with multiple cot deaths, convicted under the 'one cot death an accident, two suspicious and three murder' dictat of one man. Who knows what other, undiscovered rare abnormalities are lurking? I just think how terribly, terribly lucky we have been not to have had three cot deaths – Art, if he'd vomited one more time, Ella, if I'd held off the bottle one more day, and, of course, Frank, if he'd slept peacefully for another hour or so. So no, feeding them a few glucose drinks and admitting them occasionally is not a problem at all. Dr. Jones said we were unlucky having three children affected, but we haven't been unlucky at all. We have been very, very lucky. We have three healthy children. I am not in jail for their murder. And we know what to do when they are ill.

The worst side effect of the MCAD was that Ella had to have regular feeds, and she couldn't be allowed to sleep more than four hours at a time. For the first time in my life, I had a baby who slept and had to commit the number one heinous crime of parenting: waking a sleeping baby. And, of course, if you wake a baby up, it doesn't feel like breastfeeding. I won't bore you with another long tizz over breastfeeding again, but suddenly, two months later, it sorted itself out. I was a breastfeeding mother! I could therefore excuse myself all other parenting sins from now until my dying day.

"The one thing I do recommend is breastfeeding, because no matter how much of a mess your house is, or however else you may fail to be a perfect parent, you can stand up and say – 'I breastfed my baby'". Libby Purves from *How Not To Be A Perfect Mother* (adapted from memory, I've lost the actual book in my messy house!)

Great advice – except, of course, if you can't breastfeed. Anyway, God had decided to give me a break and I could breastfeed! Now I could look smugly at those mothers bottle-feeding their babies and think – *Breast is Best*, don't you know?

* **To any new mums**

MCAD is very, very, very rare (about one in 13,000). Adrenoleucodystrophy is even rarer (1 in 10 million). Your child's lifetime risk of being struck by lightning is greater than both of these. Cot death frightens us so because there is so little else that our Western children die of, but it too is very rare (about 0.6 per 1,000) and is getting rarer, so please don't worry. And although it sticks in my craw to say it, *Breast is Best* and is worth giving your every effort. But what you need is HELP. Midwives, breastfeeding counsellors, doulas, a pal down the road to help with the actual technique, and as much help as you possibly can lay your hands on for everything else in the house, so you can sleep as much as possible during the day. Pay for it if you have to (if you are at all able to afford it). Find out who the breastfeeding counsellors etc are in your area, before you have a baby, in the event of you needing help. Remember, there are some lucky so-and-so's who take to it immediately, no trouble at all, and they just can't understand why some find it so difficult. What I say is that some people are good at maths/tennis/drawing/dancing/boxing/breastfeeding. There are also those who are genetically unable, for example, to roll their tongue. Nobody would call those that *can* roll their tongues morally superior, would they?

There are ways round feeding a child in the early days, such as finger feeding (you squirt milk in with a syringe as they suck on your finger) which gets round the nipple/teat confusion thing, which is often a problem. (See addendum on Chapter 8 for references).

The moral of this story is not to worry what may go wrong (because if you are alive, things will go wrong somewhere down the line), because while you're busy worrying about x going wrong, you're busy not noticing y going wrong under your very nose. Do follow your instincts , however. I knew TWICE in a fortnight, that something was wrong with first Frank then baby Ella, but failed to act. It's nothing to do with being a doctor. I think mothers do know when something is really not right.

17. Life's Too Short.

To Sit In A Traffic Jam

Stress *stres, n.*
...physical, emotional or mental strain;
the system of forces applied to a body;
emphasis.

Why are we all so stressed these days? Are there more physical, emotional or mental forces being applied to us, or is it that we are putting too much emphasis on the inevitable strains of life that we are all subjected to?

Dr. Maslow has a lot to answer for. All those needs you never even knew were needs, all those expectations of a perfect person, all that dissatisfaction from not reaching the upper rungs. Maslow's hierarchy was supposed to be for needs, but I think his higher rungs are just great big unfulfilled wants.

We're stressed because we're obsessed with choice. The more there is to choose from, the more we start wondering if we are giving the right emphasis to our choices. And the more choices there are, the more things there are to want.

When my Dad said (and everyone else's Dad too, no doubt) "I want never gets," it didn't take long for me to learn to say please. Now I want, and 90 percent of the time, I get. And can I accept that other ten percent that I don't get, even though I said pretty please ever so nicely, without needing reminding at all? No. I cannot. I want it all. Then, much of the time, when I get it, I decide I don't want it any more.

"Want that...don't want it." Matt Lucas, *Little Britain*

"Do not spoil what you have by desiring what you have not." Epicurus 300 B.C.

Even the Rolling Stones had the same idea:

"You can't always get what you want... but if you try sometime, you just might find, you get what you need."

Other than the very few landed aristocracy, warlords or tribal leaders, it's only very recently that most of us humans have had all that much choice. Then, with our economic surplus (and this is how we judge a country's success?), the explosion of the media and internet, we are bombarded with more and more choices. And are we grateful for all this choice? No, we either just complain that our particular choice isn't on the menu, or get stressed over all these damned choices and decisions we have to make.

I was a lot less stressed in my time in Sierra Leone, despite suffering from unrequited love, despite trying to do things way beyond my capabilities and despite the early rebel invasion. (Later when things got really bad, there was fear, not stress). I was a lot less stressed because I wasn't overwhelmed with choice. Every day I ate mashed leaf and dried fish cooked in oil, served on rice. I might choose whether or not to have a banana, orange or handful of peanuts that day, and if so, how many. I didn't have to agonise over how to treat my patients. Either I could help, or I couldn't. I would only attempt to operate, for instance, if they would die if I didn't. Even my 'choice' of unrequited love was the only eligible bachelor at the time. When the rebels came, I had to choose whether to stay or go, but in the end the choice was made for me (a choice not available to the local people).

But of course, the main reason I was less stressed in Sierra Leone was that I only had to worry about my own stomach, and my own physical and emotional well-being. Now I have a string of little stomachs and the physical and emotional well-being of three developing egos.

Having said that, now we'd both got the hang of breastfeeding, Ella's stomach was filling up nicely. The boys were happily settled in school and playgroup, burying the house in paintings, drawing and complex cardboard box models, and they loved Ella, their heart-stoppingly beautiful angel sister, who smiled, gurgled and slept. Oh, the bliss of a sleeping baby! The winter passed really quite peacefully and we managed several months in a row without a major disaster. Uncle Mick finally got some treatment and he responded really well, so Grandma Peg was able to go in to get her deferred knee replacement, so she wasn't in so much pain all the time.

I went back to work without any great drama and even attended a lecture on stress.

The Holmes and Rahe Social Readjustment Scale

(1967)

The speaker handed us all a stress scale to fill in. The Holmes and Rahe Social Readjustment Scale scores 43 different life events with ratings (another hierarchy!) according to what they considered the likely life impact. For example:

100 – death of a spouse
73 – divorce
65 – other relationship breakdowns
63 – jail term
63 – death of a close family member
60 – menopause
50 – marriage
39 – birth
40 – pregnancy
28 – outstanding personal achievement
25 – less than eight hours sleep
15 – change in eating habits (another good reason not to
    go on a diet)
13 – holiday
12 – Christmas

Plus all sorts of other things like loss of jobs, status, finances. As you can see, not all of these are 'adverse' life events.

You score yourself as to how stressed you are:

Under 150 - Be glad (37 percent chance of a serious illness, mental or physical, in the next two years)
150 - 300 - Be cautious (51 percent chance of serious illness)
> 300 - Be very careful (80 percent chance of serious physical and mental illness in the next two years).

I totted up my score. 450!!! Suddenly I felt panicky. Nothing is more stressful than someone telling you you're stressed. You too can make yourself feel more stressed by downloading similar score sheets from the internet. Of course these are usually attached to various stress-relieving products for sale, or a little box at the bottom: 'click here for a therapist', so they have a vested interest in overestimating your stress. These scores can be confusing, depending on when you count these life event units over the past two years, or just one year, or only six months. And some things you can count twice, like pregnancy usually results in 'another member of the family' and probably in an 'outstanding personal achievement' and it certainly results in 'less than eight hours sleep a night.' Really, once you start putting 'Christmas – 12 points' and 'holidays – 13 points', then you measure it for over a two year period and you've gone over the first threshold for just living! To be stressed is to be alive.

How much worse is it if you don't have anything happening in your life to register a score? Dr. Kyriazis, Director of the British Longevity Society, suggests that stress keeps us young, and suggests therapies like redecorating your living room in a weekend, or not leaving enough time to pack for a trip overseas. Fantastic, I'll never need botox! But loneliness and loss of purpose must be the greatest stress of all.

Amah never really recovered from Ahcong's death. They had been together since primary school, and how do you suddenly cope, alone at eighty-five, after seventy-five years together? That's real stress. How can loss of a spouse only be counted as a mere 100 points, the equivalent score of seven holidays?

Only a few years ago, well into her eighties, Amah would make homemade mincemeat, bramble jelly, sloe gin, shortbread and magnificent meals for the whole Global Family as they returned for Christmas. When she wasn't cooking or baking, Amah delivered meals on wheels to the 'old folk'. For the last few years of Ahcong's life, she looked after him, lovingly, tirelessly, uncomplaining day and night. But one day Ahcong was gone, and she was left alone, her purpose gone, hundreds of miles from the rest of her family. Life is not meant to be lived alone. Amah stopped cooking. Now the shop in the Square delivered her a cling-filmed sandwich and a packet of prawn cocktail crisps. We still visited, with each new baby and when holidays allowed ,for the fifteen hour round trip. But we had our own life and stresses to contend with. People always do. And unlike Sierra Leone (sorry to bang on about it, it's just an example), here in the 'civilised' world we have to cope with our stresses in isolation from the rest of our family.

Amah finally moved to Allanbank to be near my Mum, leaving Monikie, their magnificent Victorian house in Strathfarrell standing empty. I know a house doesn't fulfill any of my definitions of life, but it still needs we humans to care for it, or it will rot and decay. Monikie was crying out for life to fill it once more. Crying out for us to fill it, joked Danny.

Reasons to be Grateful, Part 22

Move to Monikie? Hmmm. No, don't be daft. A soul needs a body in which to live, a virus needs a cell, a snail needs its shell and we humans need a home. But we already had a perfectly good home! Our house in Boldham fulfilled all of Maslow's needs: shelter, warmth, belonging (great friends and nice neighbours), a bit of self-actualising art work on the walls and a bit of beauty with a nice view over a field of sheep. Uncle Rod had built us a fantastic conservatory (excellent for train tracks and wind up toys), giving us an even better view of the sheep.

One function our house hadn't fulfilled so well (and a bottom rung function too) was sleep. It was built before building regulations stipulated a certain thickness of wall, and after the days when they just built nice thick walls anyway, out of a sense of pride or decency. So when Art cried, night after night as a baby, there was no room unpenetrated by the piercing, stomach-churning noise, even after Uncle Rod added an extra six inches of polystyrene soundproofing between Art's bedroom and ours.

Listen to me! Talk about ingratitude. Optimists don't complain! The reality was we had a lovely house (not as nice as Monikie, though) and Art's poor sleep was all in the past. Frank was never too bad a sleeper, other than his *joie de vivre* bursting into the new day at half past five in the morning, and we were blessed with Ella (see, I just knew a girl would sleep better), who slept too well.

So, nice house, good friends, Danny's family an hour away and good jobs. Admittedly, Danny's enthusiasm for tracing the movements of large wads of money through technological mazes had waned somewhat, as had his patience for long traffic jams, but it was a good job. And I loved my practice, for all I moaned about having to juggle childcare. What were we thinking of, moving to Monikie, even as a joke? Optimists should think their grass is plenty green enough, thank you. What would we do? Just turn up in the Highlands with two little boys, a baby, two dogs and no job between us and marvel at the three foot solid stone walls and handsome green gables?

Stress = Loss of Control

Workers can cope with very demanding jobs as long as they feel that they have some level of control. I've felt stressed at work, of course: too many patients, too little time. Or sometimes just one humdinger of a patient, who makes your pulse race and your teeth grit, just by seeing their name in the appointment list. A properly poorly patient or an actual emergency is generally fine

– adrenaline rush stress lifts you up, rather than the depressing gnaw of 'can't cope' stress.

Of course I really had no idea about real stress until I had children. It's all those variables, the lack of control, and those unrealistic expectations. Like wanting a bit of time for ourselves, for instance. I expect some time for myself, then I get stressed when I don't get it. If I do get ten minutes or even an hour, I get stressed that I don't feel relaxed at the end of it, or that I haven't made the most of it. For heaven's sake! I just shouldn't expect so much, then I wouldn't feel so frustrated. These happy years, busy years, with our children are spoilt because we've seen too much stuff about the hard working mother juggling children and responsibilities etc. etc. And it won't be for ever (please tell me it won't be forever!) We're told we're out of control and stressed, so we feel out of control. Of course we probably are out of control, but my point is, so what? The problem is that we expect to be in control in the first place.

I always felt much more in control at work than at home (which is infinitely harder than work). The 'working' bit of working mum remained fine, it was being the 'mum' bit as well that was the problem. The 'mum' part had to be covered by super-flexi childcare arrangements of full-time school, part-time school, part-time nursery, a few hours from Katrina and notching up an enormous brownie point deficit with various friends. All just about manageable when everything goes smoothly, but 'life goes smoothly' isn't a phrase anybody suggested when I asked for their definition of life. If life can go wrong, it will (and if nothing had gone wrong then we would never have climbed out of the primordial soup).

The more variables there are the more likely my flexi, flexi, what-way-up-am-I-today? childcare arrangements were likely to fall apart. Variables are of course exponentially related to the number of children. Too many children, not enough time.

As anyone with children knows, your arrangements collapse when anyone is ill, even if your children don't have some funny genetic disease. Then to make it worse they either all go down with the same thing together, or, more inconveniently, fall sick like dominos (usually infecting parents and childminders as they go).

And it's usually at the most inconvenient time, like Charles being on holiday, leaving me as the only doctor at West Hill Surgery.

Sick = I.M.P.O.S.S.I.B.L.E.

Publicly, I would groan about my full time stints for Charles' holidays, but secretly I quite liked it. Full time was actually much easier. You didn't have to cram everything into two or three days, so at least I felt in control at work and you just had to leave looking after the children to someone else. All very fine until Ella needed to go into hospital (the MCAD equation – Poorly+Not Feeding = Glucose Drip). Danny had already missed so much work with Frank's coma, then Ella's birth, visiting Mick whilst he had his chemotherapy and visiting his mum in hospital after her knee replacement. Anyway, I was still breastfeeding, so in I had to go, leaving Sue (our magnificent Practice Nurse/Practice Manager/personal nanny/childminder/counsellor/dog-sitter/fixer of cars and computers) holding the fort. Fortunately, Sue loved nothing more than a good crisis to sort out (stress certainly kept Sue young). After virtually no sleep, I staggered back to work to a surgery of postponed patients and a backlog of paperwork. I had just about caught up when five days later, Frank was poorly too and in he had to go. Let's just rename the Children's Ward of Boldham District Hospital 'the Pike Wing'.

Using my years of medical training, I have worked out a formula for the chance of your children getting sick.

S (sick) = I.M.P.O.S.S.I.B.L.E where:
I = important things the parent must do
M = Medic in the household (nothing like having a doctor or a nurse as a parent to bring home the germs along with the bacon)
P = Parent is poorly themselves
O = your other children have been poorly
S = number of other children at school or nursery, thus picking up germs
S = number of siblings
I = pre-existing illness in child (e.g.: MCAD)

B = bugs and beasties doing the rounds in the community
L = other, unaccounted for, random life event
E = level of pre-existing exhaustion in parent

This was bloody impossible! What was I doing? What was life about? Never mind the whole of life, what was my life about? What did I really want? More time with my children, a happy marriage (requiring a happy husband, which was unlikely when he was spending half his life frustrated over office politics, or computers that didn't do what they were meant to, or sat in a traffic jam). What else? More time to write, less form filling, some time with patients under my own control, a beautiful, toned body, eternal happiness, spiritual satisfaction, endless food and drink without putting on weight. Oh, and world peace and making enough money to rebuild Serabu Hospital in Sierra Leone on the massive proceeds from the royalties of *Green Oranges*. What was I saying earlier about realistic expectations?

A few weeks after Charles returned from holiday, he handed me a coffee and said that he'd been approached with a merger offer by another, much bigger, GP practice. What did I think? Gosh. Merge?

Charles' argument made a lot of sense. There was the dreaded new GP contract looming, for starters. Returning to work with three children, the new GP contract was one thing I refused to worry about, so I instituted a quite successful policy of leaving as much of the managerial stuff to the (ever-so-slight) control-freakery of Charles and Sue. Then there was our surgery building. Totally unsuitable. Much as we loved West Hill, it was wearing to have to play musical rooms if I needed to see a patient who couldn't make it up the stairs. Then the Boldham Council refused us planning for a disabled ramp to our front door (!*@%$!), leaving the only disabled access via the back alley, intermittently sprinkled with broken heroin ampoules, needles and broken bottles from our bail hostel neighbours. And we couldn't afford a new build in central Boldham on our own. Deep down I knew I couldn't really argue against a merger, but the thought of leaving our cosy two partner practice, where the receptionists were on first name terms with everyone, to a huge conglomerate health centre, no matter how shiny and new, staffed no doubt by the sort of receptionists that would force patients to come in to see the doctor less than a day after having a baby, or not pass messages on to the doctors who were just far too busy to actually sort out a sick patient, secretly appalled me.

The next day, after school, I took the children to the park opposite Frank's old nursery, the one that used to make hot toast and was forced to shut down. Frank had just started school. "That's my nursery! I want to see my nursery!" yelped Frankie. It was nearly two years since he'd been there, I was amazed he remembered, but he was so persistent that I took him over to have a look. All boarded up. Very sad.

"I liked my nursery, Mummy. Why can't I go there any more?"

"Because it's closed, darling. And anyway, you're a big boy and you go to school now."

"But school's not fun," moaned my four year old.

Oh Frankie, who said life's about having fun? You're four now, you're not allowed any fun any more.

When did life become such a chore? Whatever had happened to me?

Dancing with the Downsizers

My Holmes and Rahe stress rating remained well over 300, and I was still standing, but for how much longer? You've seen all the advice, dished out on a daily basis in all the magazines, lifestyle section of the papers, shelves of self-help books, half of cyber-space and even by me to my own patients: follow your dreams, do it now, life's too short, be true to yourself etc., etc. After our near death experience with Frank, all the children diagnosed with a potentially fatal condition, and Mick's scare with throat cancer, life might indeed be a lot shorter than you bargained for. So we would be true to ourselves, follow our dreams and do it. We would ditch all our stress and go for that elusive 'quality of life'. We would move to Monikie where the air was fresh, the scenery beautiful and the cars few and free-flowing. Even the dogs would love it (okay, anthropomorphism, they're just dumb dogs with no opinion), but I could see them now, bounding freely over the hill, the wind in their floppy black spaniel ears.

We would go North. We would dance with the downsizers (well, Monikie is not what you'd call downsizing). We'd worry about small details like jobs later.

life *laif, n.* a chance

Don't waste it.

18. Your Life in Their Hands

Then Mick got poorly again. False hopes lie on the darker side of optimism. Bad things happen, no matter how we may hope or believe that they won't. Optimists don't complain, but frankly Mick had a really bad time. I'd like to give a more positive spin on things, and praise the great NHS, my employer, but I can't. There was the six month delay before he was even diagnosed, and that was only because he presented himself to Casualty, choking. God, was it really that long? I knew I wasn't exempt from guilt here, either. I should have intervened earlier, but I was too caught up in my own problems, too respectful of my colleagues and too optimistic that the system I worked in had its failings but could always pull itself together for an emergency. Then Mick was taunted with false hopes, pretending he didn't have cancer after all, just the (very rare) benign pharyngeal pouch. I assumed that having made such a cock-up of the diagnosis (unfair of me to say that, it happens), they would try especially hard for him thereafter. Cruel optimism.

Well, this is how it went. Just after Ella was born, Mick was finally sent for an MRI scan. The MRI showed that the cancer was spreading from his throat and around the spine in his neck - in other words, inoperable. For some reason, even though Mick was an inpatient on the ward, the Consultant, Mr. J., arranged to see Mick in Outpatients to tell him the news wasn't good. Mick ended up waiting all afternoon in the crowded Outpatients for a late running clinic to hear the news that was so 'not good' that Mick probably only had two months to live. Why on Earth couldn't Mr. J. have taken Mick aside into a quiet room on the ward to tell him such news, rather than subjecting him to the torture of hanging around all afternoon in a busy clinic?

Mick took the news very well. Unfortunately, he wasn't at all surprised. Then Mr. J. decided that since Mick was a single parent to a teenage son, he'd refer him up to Mr. C., for a super-specialist opinion: "Mick deserved to have all the stops pulled out in his situation."

'All the stops' meant a three week wait for Mr. C.

Mr. C. was very professional, very thorough and told Mick he'd like to do his own endoscopy to see for himself if anything was technically, surgically, possible. I thought that the MRI had already told us that surgery wasn't possible, but Mr. C. was the specialist and maybe, just maybe...

There was another two week wait to be admitted for the second endoscopy, which failed. "There's too much blockage," said Mr. C.

I'm sorry, but there was too much blockage for them to do it last time and without any treatment, the blockage was only ever going to get worse. Mr. C. decided to put Mick to sleep and try another endoscopy under anaesthetic so he could take some more biopsies. Why? Was he expecting it suddenly not to be cancerous any more? Mr. C. said he'd send Mick another outpatient appointment to discuss the biopsy results. Two weeks later, Mick still hadn't heard, so we rang up, and got fitted in for the next again week. At this appointment Mr. C. said it was inoperable – because you could see it had spread round the spine on the MRI scan. Well, we knew that eight weeks ago. Mr. C. surely knew that eight weeks ago too, when he saw the original scans when Mr. J. had referred him? Well no, he hadn't actually seen the scans. Well surely Mr. J. had sent him the report? Yes, said Mr. C., he had seen the report, but he liked to look at the scans himself. Fine. Well why didn't you bloody well look then? Eight weeks ago.

Of course I never said it quite like this. Too bloody polite, and I wasn't sure it would help Mick to shove all this bureaucratic incompetency over his life under his nose. He had enough to cope with. Anyway Mr. C. said he'd refer Mick to the oncologists so they could consider chemotherapy and radiotherapy. Sometimes that could shrink it down enough so it might be operable at a later date. So Mr. C. wrote a referral letter to Dr. M. And yes, there was another two weeks plus before he could see Dr. M. A total of eleven weeks wait for a man who'd been told at the beginning that two months was a best guess prognosis. The only treatment Mick had had was the feeding tube Mr. J. had inserted directly into Mick's stomach the day after he was admitted.

The feeding tube was hidden under Mick's shirt, but Mick hated it. It made him feel like a freak. But there was no alternative. Mick couldn't even swallow his beer or tea, and beer and tea were Mick's greatest pleasures in life. Other than cigarettes, which probably no longer gave quite so much enjoyment.

Mick was finally admitted by Dr. M. for chemotherapy the week before Christmas. By this time, he had developed an aspiration pneumonia from his choking attacks and was no longer fit for the chemo. Dr. M. allowed Mick home for Christmas Day, on large doses of antibiotics. We all went round to Peg and Bob's, sort of for a last Christmas for Mick, I suppose, and we were all desperate to make it a good one. Not very easy, with Mick coughing, at times choking, struggling for his breath as the tumour started to impinge on his windpipe.

Mick was always very good with babies and children and cuddled the fourteen week Ella briefly, but although she smiled gratifyingly up at the kind face of her uncle, he soon handed her back, self-conscious, I think, about her lying across the feeding tube site. Mick obviously wasn't going to manage turkey, Christmas pud, a glass of wine, beer or a wee dram, as he couldn't even swallow his saliva. And Peg and Bob's house wasn't very big, so five extra Pikes round the table put up in the sitting room, left Mick nowhere much to go but the kitchen full of Christmas dinner debris, or the spare bedroom. He chose the bedroom. Would you want to watch everyone else eat?

What do you get a man who's terminally ill for Christmas? Pyjamas, sheets and a dressing gown was what lay under the tree for Mick – how awful. So I asked him. Mick wanted cigarettes. So for the first time in my entire life (yes, I was one of those ghastly self-righteous children who hid or burned her mother's cigarettes, or filled the packets with little notes saying 'it's bad for you'), I bought cigarettes. Two hundred of them, smuggled into the house so Danny and his parents wouldn't see. I'd once been sent a letter from a hospital doctor about one of my patients. The last line was "I have strongly advised this man to stop smoking". The man in question was a heroin addict for many, many years, who knocked back large quantities of whisky and beer, and was in his last months of life, dying of cancer. Anyway, "Too bloody late to give up now" was my patient's rather reasonable response. Not that this stopped the overwhelming feeling of guilt as I handed over the cigarette money at the kiosk, like I was shop-lifting or buying porno-mags or something. Mick thanked me for his present and smiled. First time in ages.

Mick finally got treatment in the New Year and it was almost miraculous. By Easter, Mick could swallow again and he celebrated the removal of the hated feeding tube with a pint of beer. He could have his cup of tea, his beer and even smoke his cigarettes without coughing. Mick even started talking about giving them up. It was in this window of hope that I handed my notice into Charles and we put our house on the market. Peg even got her knee replaced and Danny was back in hospital visiting his Mum. "In the last four months I've been in hospitals with my son, my wife, my brother and my Mum, I'm sick of bloody hospitals."

But it was too soon for Danny to make jovial comments. It was also too soon for us to sell our house. Mick was choking on his tea again. His tumour was back, and worse. We couldn't leave now, so we moved into rented accommodation, the dogs into kennels and tenants into Monikie.

Chemo and radiotherapy tends not to work so well the second time and Mick was no exception. Soon he was struggling even to breath. It was like each step on Maslows's hierarchy was being pulled from under him. Safety, food, water, and even breathing.

All that was left was his self-esteem. Mick had had his problems in the past, but boy, was he being stoic about all this.

So the feeding tube had to go back in and then when Mick couldn't lie down, or even just recline in a chair for a rest without choking, Mr. J put in an artificial windpipe – a tracheotomy tube. Oxygen, oxygen, oxygen. The tracheotomy certainly improved his colour, his breathing and reduced the terrifying choking episodes, but Mick hated it even more than the feeding tube.

The tumour started bleeding, worsened by the friction from the tracheotomy tube. The specialist tracheotomy nurse came, and tried shorter, longer, narrower, wider, softer, firmer versions. One morning a blood clot blocked the tracheotomy tube, leaving my 77 year old father in law, who was himself suffering from a nasty arthritic condition that required high dose steroids, with a panic-stricken drive to the hospital; Mick, his son, gasping in the front seat.

Bob then learned to change Mick's tracheotomy tube himself. He would do it in the kitchen, which was already small, but now filled with the paraphernalia of the ill: liquid feeds piled high next to Peg and Bob's cornflakes, tracheotomy tubes and dressings in a large cardboard box sitting on the ironing board, bottles of medication and syringes lined up on the fridge next to the two for one teabags and cut price apple pie and the specially baked Hedon bread cakes. Not that Mick would ever have apple pie, bread cakes or even tea again.

Finally they seemed to get the tube right and Mick was looking better. Bob got out for the first time in months, to see Hedon City play in their new home ground. Hedon City won, but unfortunately Bob tripped over a loose kerb as the triumphant crowd exited the stadium from watching their team's victory. Poor Bob. He had cracked several ribs, could hardly take a proper breath for the pain, and was bruised from his neck to his waist, made worse by the steroids he was already taking for his arthritis. Mick had to go to the hospice to be looked after until Bob was better.

Bob did get better, and Mick seemed to get better too. He was due to go back home to Peg and Bob's on the Monday, and looked better than he had in ages, but he died on the Sunday morning. Quite peacefully in the end. Mick lost the ability to eat, drink, and finally breathe.

On the Tuesday morning the tracheotomy nurse came to the house, with a student in tow, to make sure Bob knew how to change Mick's new tracheotomy tube.

Before Mick died, Danny and I wondered if we should submit an official complaint for the catalogue of delays. Given Mick's remarkable, if short-lived, response to the radiotherapy and chemotherapy, perhaps he could have been granted a few more years (perhaps even a cure?) if he'd been treated promptly. I wasn't keen. How does money compensate for people's lives? I generally don't like people suing doctors either, as nobody's perfect and we usually try our best with what's available. I have also seen how stressful these cases are for everyone, and in particular the patient, and thought Mick could well do without feeling dissatisfied and untrusting of the people who were still caring for him. But Mick had sought legal aid himself. He knew it would be too late for his own benefit, but he was thinking of Steve, his seventeen year old son. So Danny and I typed out reports and dates at Mick's request and all was proceeding well. Until Mick died. With the 'claimant' dead, the case apparently could not proceed, and Steve couldn't pursue the compensation on his Dad's behalf through the legal aid system because he was under-age. Danny sought further legal advice, but the specialist report stated that there was no case to answer; it was impossible to prove that Mick would have been cured if he had been treated earlier, nor was it possible to prove that he had been complaining of difficulty swallowing for six months before he was finally seen by a specialist (never mind the further three months before he was actually treated) because it wasn't noted in the GP's records. So the GP had effectively defended himself by keeping bad records. The best defence is silence indeed.

Sometimes it's hard to be an optimist.

19. Life at a Higher Latitude

Downsizing

"There are so many things I can do without." Socrates

"Nothing lasts. Suffering comes from being attached to the things of ordinary existence." Buddha

Is downsizing the answer to climbing the pyramid? Escape the rat race to the Highlands for a stress-free life? Relax into a quieter way of life, into the arms of time, beckoning we lost souls to rediscover our brains and our creativity? Who were we kidding? Your life follows you wherever you go.

Unfortunately, our journey to stress-less bliss would have to start with that well known relaxation activity. Moving house.

Moving House - 50 points?

Sometime before Mick died we made our decision to move. We couldn't wait in limbo any longer and at that point he was relatively stable, our six month lease was up, the dogs were languishing in kennels at great cost, we'd both resigned our jobs and we'd already deferred the boys starting their new school by first one, then two terms. It was time to move.

On our 'last' day in Boldham we drove through to the Hedon Hospice to see Mick, who was looking forward to getting home on the Monday now his Dad's fractured ribs were healing. Frankie and Art kissed their Uncle. Mick gave them a thumbs up and Ella a cuddle, mouthing "see you" as we left.

Danny and Frankie stayed that Saturday night with Peg and Bob, so Danny could visit Mick again that evening. I went back to Boldham and my parents helped me pack up the hired transit van, ready for the long journey on the Sunday. We'd already sent up ninety-nine packing boxes of stuff and loads of furniture up to Monikie (all of which we'd managed perfectly well without).

Having squeezed everything into the van, we had no pots or pans, so my parents bought us an Indian carry-out which we ate on the floor, drank lagers from the bottle and went to sleep on mattresses on the floor.

The telephone woke us at 7.30 a.m. It was Danny from the hospice. Mick had died in the early hours.

I drove straight to Peg and Bob's, just to be there, but also to collect Frankie. In between making lots of cups of tea, I tried to phone the estate agent on their emergency number to extend our rental by a couple of weeks. They made one or two apologetic noises, but refused even a single extra day, saying they had to show more people round on Monday afternoon. So I had to leave Danny in Hedon and drive back to Boldham with the children. Thank goodness for my Mum and Dad who came to the rescue and drove our furniture van up to Strathfarrell, and my friends indeed, Katrina and Sam. Katrina took the boys to the park for a few hours, leaving Sam to help me clean the house of all sticky handprints on the walls, windows and cupboards (and try to prevent Ella from creating more).

Whilst I waited for Danny to get back from Hedon on the Monday morning, I visited the post office to re-route the mail, then took the old mattresses and about ten black bags of junk to the city dump. I returned, Ella writhing in arms, to find the estate agent grilling Danny for the 'final inspection'. She tapped her officious clipboard and went on and on about a few tiny marks on the wall and a stain on the carpet which had been under our double bed. She was still complaining about a few dandelions in the back flower bed when the funeral director rang for Danny. It's not often that I lose my temper, it really isn't, but I really, really wanted to punch her pretty, powdered nose. I really did. I wonder if she was related to those receptionists? Those people who are all clipboard and no heart. Anyway, Danny sorted out a time for the cremation, whilst I slapped the keys on top of the woman's clipboard and we were left standing in the drive with Ella crying for her lunch, homeless.

Peg and Bob's two-up two-down council house in Hedon is perfect for the two of them, but hardly suitable for an extra five of us and two dogs crammed into Mick's room, now sadly just 'the spare room', still full of dressings, medicines, tracheotomy tubes and liquid feed. We decided that Danny would stay with his parents with one child at a time for 'cheering up purposes' and I would camp out at friends' houses with the other two and drive through to Hedon each day for a child swap. Fortunately, the nice lady in the kennels was not related to aforesaid receptionist and squeezed Rogie and Bo in as extras for two more weeks.

On the day of the funeral, I was back staying with Charles and Ruth (and what good friends they turned out to be, despite all Charles' aversion to touchy-feeliness) with Ella and Frank. The funeral was at 9.15 a.m. in Hedon, a good hour away. There were mutterings from some of the family that Danny had arranged the funeral too damned early in the morning and too soon 'just to suit us, because we were moving' (people always have to complain about something). But the funeral was on Maunday Thursday, four days later (a perfectly respectable wait in Scotland) and if it wasn't then it would have been another five days to clear the Easter break.

Anyway it was at 9.15 a.m., the only time the crematorium could offer us, which was of course, too bloody early, but at least it meant Peg didn't have to spend all morning fretting, and that working people could come and get back to work (if they so wanted). It was just a bit of a problem for me to get a four year old and a toddler from Boldham to Peg and Bob's at rush hour. I allowed an hour and a half. This might have been okay had Ella not been up all night with a high temperature and not feeding. With the MCAD problem, I should have admitted her to hospital, but felt I really should get to the funeral, so instead of a glucose drip, I stuffed her full of lucozade and calpol. Now spending the night stuffing a feverish one year old full of lucozade and paracetamol syrup, then waking her up at six a.m. (when she's only just dropped off), to ram her first into a posh dress, then into a car, is a recipe for an enormous vomit on the side of the dual carriageway. So, whilst cars sped heartlessly past to work, off comes Ella's posh dress and on goes backup dress. Unfortunately *I* didn't have a backup dress (all packed up and driven up to Scotland), so the splodge of sick on my shoulder that refused to come off with the baby wipe would just have to stay. Ram poorly child back in car seat, tell 'not poorly' four year old to shut up, yes, we are nearly there, then arrive just as Danny and Art, Rod, Peg and Bob were getting into the car. Danny scooped Frank up and called out directions to me as they drove off. I fumbled round Peg and Bob's small bathroom, trying to extinguish any last sick smells from both me and Ella, chanced it with another dose of paracetamol syrup, and raided Peg's airing cupboard for some emergency towels.

Finding the crematorium was another problem. Danny's directions seemed clear enough at the time, but pre-supposed a partial knowledge of Hedon. I took a wrong turning, got stuck at a railway level crossing, had to do a U turn, got stuck again, and arrived at the Chapel of Rest in time for the closing bars of *Let it Be*.

Ella and I squeezed into a pew at the back. Within minutes, Ella was objecting, so I carried her out, just as Danny stood up to give his eulogy. I tried to keep Ella quiet with some vigorous jiggling so I could listen to Danny's tribute to his big brother through the crack in the door, but no, Ella was having none of it. If jiggled any harder, she would be sick again, so I hoiked her fold-away buggy out of the car, and wheeled her for a few loops round the memorial garden. It was, at least, a beautiful day and the daffodils were out. I do like daffodils. Isn't yellow just a great colour?

Ten days later, once we decided Peg and Bob were 'bearing up', we finally packed up the children and the dogs and arrived at Monikie, more stressed than ever. Of course, none of this would even register on any worldwide scale of disasters, but I recalculated my life units on the Holmes and Rahe stress score for soft Westerners: moving house (twice), loss of jobs, change in financial status, death of close family member, trying to make new friends and networks for us and the children (there's points for all that sort of thing too) and still well less than eight hours sleep. There didn't seem to be any points awarded for your little angel baby morphing into a Terrible Toddler, which surely must score at least 50, nor for your dog having a nervous breakdown (poor old Rogie). Not including these last two, I'll just add that up ... 360! And we don't even have any proper problems!

There's a children's scale, slightly adapted to include things like changing school, exams and parental divorce, but there must be some mathematical correlation between a child's stress and their parents'. Perhaps there's a doggy scale too?

Rogie Rogues

Taking an optimistic view, I suppose we were lucky that Rogie was the only one of the family to have a nervous breakdown.

What can I say about Rogie? Our beautiful, beautiful boy, soft and stupid, our Pedigree Chump, our lovable woofter who had never really ever learnt to water a lamppost. I think he had actually quite liked being in kennels. He still had his beloved Bo, and a nice lady who loved him, and all that lovely routine. The kennels had been a good thing for Bo's arthritic hip too, as it meant we could enforce her diet. We were very impressed when we took her to the vet for a weigh-in.

"Half a stone! For a dog! Well done Bo."

"Shall we just check Rogie, too?" suggested the vet.

"Rogie? But we haven't had Rogie on a diet."

"I just thought he was looking a bit thin."

"Yes, now you mention it ... he's so hairy I hadn't really noticed...Over a stone! Oh Rogie!"

It wasn't just the weight loss, for as soon as we got to Monikie, Rogie was sniffing, sniffing, sniffing, round and round the garden in an interminable loop, until his nose bled and the grass was bare. Always the same loop, even if we were with him throwing sticks and balls. What was he sniffing for? Love probably. Or next-door's black cat. Somewhere between Boldham, the kennels and the Highlands, our soft mutt had developed a blood lust for felines and the merest glimpse of the black mog (or any other) and Rogie would forget his 'circuit' and vanish out of the garden and into the village, his barks echoing up the valley. Clearly we needed a gate.

Four hundred and fifty pounds that gate cost us. The fencer was just tidying away his tools when Rogie spotted the black mog and with a hop, skip and a jump he cleared the new gate. The fencer climbed into his truck and made some comment about Rogie's athletic prowess. Yeah, great. Rogie was always a fit dog, but Bo's diet had transformed him into a honed, toned lean, greyhound that could now leap a five foot fence. I tried chasing him, calling his name but after three children and a lot of comfort eating, there was no way I was going to catch this mercurial beast, and there was the small matter of three unattended small children in the garden. At least we had the new gate, I thought, returning out of puff (only minutes later) to spot Ella, aged 18 months, perched at the top of the gate and swinging her leg down the other side to freedom whilst two small boys sat, singing, framing the escape route on each gatepost. Four hundred and fifty pounds well spent, then.

The vet suggested the dog psychologist, who said Rogie needed more attention and possibly even anti-depressants. No, go on, laugh. But it was obvious Rogues was a poor attention deprived beast, or at least, not the attention he wanted (ie: not a toddler sitting on his back pulling his ears).

Poor Rogie Rogues.

We tried to give him more attention, but I was doing locums all over the Highlands, never quite knowing where I would be working from one week to the next, then a child was poorly, then another, then, oh, we just couldn't cope with a needy dog. So, tearfully (but not without a big sigh of relief) we gave him away to a family that could give him the intensive one on one love that he needed. After all, Rogie was a beautiful boy.

Giving Rogie away was a real admission of failure, but it was the best thing for all our sanity. Within 24 hours Rogues had moved into his new master's bedroom, which was all he ever really wanted, and Bo, with her saintly tolerance for ear and tail pulling, moved herself firmly into the bosom of the family.

Sometimes I think that adopting each of our children out to a loving family would give them a better chance of sanity than having to live in the permanent war zone that is our house. But there was a famous psychologist who said that there are only two groups of children who develop personality problems: those that are abused and the children of perfect parents. So, sorry kids, we really can't risk you being subjected to perfect parenting, so you'll just have to muddle along with us.

Bo Bo

Now we had another problem. Bo was pining. She started dragging her feet and only occasionally mustered enough energy to leave her basket to roll over and have her tummy tickled. Then she started licking the coal dust from the hearth, then eating great lumps of the coal itself and chomping her way through the large pile of mud and rubble that the plumbers left for weeks outside our back door. Yum, yum, thought Bo. Dinner. We walked to school every day, past a cottage that was being refurbished by a young couple. Yum, yum, said Bo, tucking into a pile of builder's shrapnel. Pudding. I joked that Bo's concrete poos were resiting their house in our back garden.

Bo was really struggling up the hill now (not surprisingly, with half a ton of concrete in her belly) and had to sit down for a rest halfway. No, this wasn't right, this wasn't just a strange psychological manifestation of pining. Time for some medical attention.

As I explained her strange diet to the nice young vet, Bo was gnawing at the surgery wall, a rather tasty painted breeze block. Perhaps she was anaemic or something?

She sure was. Only 4.9g! (normal range 12-15g). A dog's blood indices were almost exactly the same as humans. Not so extraordinary, I suppose: life all has a common thread, common pathways and enzymes that all like to work at 37°C. Anyway. Dog or human, 4.9g was not good. There was nothing they could do, and given her rapid decline, the vet thought we would only be looking at weeks. Poor Bo Bo. Life's a bitch. The vet talked about transfusions and bone marrow biopsies. And then what? I asked. I draw the line at chemotherapy for a dog, I really do. Ghastly enough for humans, and after two years in Africa, well what can you say? How can you justify it for a dog? A silly argument, really, the money we've spent anyway on the dogs in food, bedding, kennelling and assorted vets bills would have fed half of TB ward in Serabu Hospital. And with change. But Bo was a member of our family, she was a life we loved, and one in my care (and after we'd failed so badly with Rogie ...). The vet tried with a slug of steroids instead, to 'stimulate things.' Well the steroids certainly stimulated her appetite.

Bo was always a dog ruled by her tummy, and now she was a dying dog, so frankly she could have what she wanted. Life's too short to go on a diet, especially when you are terminally ill.

Four months later Bo was still with us, and seemed to have lost the taste for interesting by-products of house refurbishment. She still got a bit breathless on the incline (well so did I) but managed to make it up the hill without sitting down. We checked her blood count again. 6.9g! Very good!

The vet scratched his head. "Well Bo seems to be better. She's looking a bit porky, though. Let's weigh her ...she's put on a stone! Tsk, tsk."

"Half a stone of concrete, perhaps?" I suggested.

"Bo's probably breathless because she's fat, not because she's anaemic."

"But I was trying to feed her up with proper food, so there'd be less room for coal. And you told me she was terminal!"

Not that I was going to sue him, like that fellow who sued his doctors for outliving his prognosis by several years. That would seem a little churlish. After all, we had another survivor, that most optimistic of beasts, the dog. A new chance for our new life?

Still Stressed

We were more stressed than ever! We thought we were being brave and intrepid (or stupid) with the downsizing game, but when we arrived in Strathfarrell, it seemed that everyone was doing it. And besides, a GP is not going to be long unemployed in the Highlands. I spent the first year doing locums all over for more hours a week than I ever worked at Boldham, leaving Danny going mad with childcare and no time to even think about looking for jobs, plus both of us completely exhausted and fractious. This wasn't the plan!

We had to regroup again, helped greatly by making some good pals, and getting childcare sorted (ish). Now I do a regular day a week as a GP, plus some out of hours work and Danny has taken a sabbatical from accounting and I.T. and gone to drama college (his left sleeve appeared on Monarch of the Glen, don't you know!). The children continue to bounce around Stathfarrell, exhausting everyone in their path. Art, aged eight, is writing a trilogy ("I'm on chapter 23 Mummy, what chapter are you on?"), Frankie is Mr. Sociable with the best smile in the world and Ella is, well, she's rather alarmingly like me and she's driving me mad!

"Honey, I've just shrunk Em!" exclaimed a friend on meeting Ella for the first time.

Life is still stressful, but it's good. It would probably be a lot less stressful if I wasn't trying to write books about stress and priorities!

Bo is keeping my feet warm as I type this in our bedroom (just don't tell Danny). Bo Bo and I are both trying to downsize. We're not on a diet exactly, as a diet would give me an extra stress score of 15 for 'change of eating habits'. We're just trying to curb greed – so a chocolate is okay, but not a box, and a biscuit is alright but not a packet. And no more Christmas turkeys and tubs of butter for you Bo Bo. For a bit of motivation (willpower is not my forte)

I'm making it a sponsored slim for Sierra Leone (sponsor me anyone?) – putting money (rather than food) where my mouth is. Or that's the theory. As I said, life's too short to go on a diet, but then it's also too short to be shopping for outsize clothes and too long to spend with painful arthritic hips.

Hmmm. Did I tell you they've opened a chocolate shop? Here in Strathfarrell? A Belgian couple, who make their own chocolates and the most velvety hot chocolate you've ever tasted. Excuse me a minute, I might just go and pay them a visit ...

Food, my favourite basic need.

Section 3

So What *Is* Life?

20. Perhaps, Perhaps, Perhaps

Funerals.

life *laif, n* the period between one's birth and one's death

"Life must be understood backwards; but it must be lived forwards." Soren Kierkegaad (1813-1855)

Life choices again. There's nothing like decisions to pile on the stress. Perhaps we should have done this or not done that. What if I'd done this, or not done that? Perhaps, perhaps, perhaps? Or, sticking with Doris Day. Que Sera, sera.

Would Socrates have been more popular if he had been good looking? If he had been popular in his own time, would he have been executed? If he hadn't been executed, then would any of us ever have heard of him?

How can you know what life is, or if you've been a success until you die?

That promotion may be the very thing that drives you to distraction and divorce. The failed IVF might save you from giving birth to Saddam Hussein, or just normal hyperactive triplets (who then drive you to distraction and divorce). Or perhaps distraction and divorce are the best things that could ever happen, leading you to discover your creative genius? Who knows? Perhaps it's that perfect health that you took for granted, that tomorrow will end in some ghastly disease, or the ghastly disease itself that brings out the best of you (and crass though this sounds, I can think of several examples). Or the saint who does umpteen marvellous deeds but dies during their one act of selfishness? What about the coward on the *The Sinking Ship* or *The Burning Building*, who barges his way onto the last lifeboat/flying fox which you just know will sink or snap? And oh, the smug satisfaction we feel, watching the well deserved sticky end. Why do we have to be so judgemental? Who knows what problems he faced in his lifetime? Maybe he had a pathological fear of water following the time he saved his entire battalion from certain drowning? Or he just had to get back to complete the last piece of the jigsaw for the vaccine for AIDS? Perhaps his lifeboat doesn't sink, and he does discover the vaccine for AIDS? So he finds the cure for AIDS, saves millions, wallows in self-important pride and kicks his wife's cat because he always hated the brute and it knocked his Nobel prize off the mantlepiece. Was that a good life or not?

Who knows? I suspect it's like all of our lives - some flashes of kindness, goodness and inspiration and some frankly pretty dodgy stuff. You could always write an autobiography (as honest as you like, but leaving out the *really* dodgy stuff) but that would only cover *"Life is the period of time from birth to the present day."* A perfectly valid definition of life, but it still doesn't tell you if you were ultimately a success.

On Roman tombstones, they kept it simple: He lived his life with passion. Or he didn't.

If you are famous or important enough, you can have a nice little summary printed out as an obituary. But for those of us who aren't famous, perhaps the best we can do is a little eulogy by our brother, or our daughter, at our funeral. That's if you have someone eloquent enough, or brave enough, to stand up in front of all those relatives without getting choked. And that's assuming you have relatives, friends or indeed, anyone at all at your funeral.

So. Funerals. I haven't been to very many. In fact, only three.

Three Funerals

1. Granny

Granny died at 84 after a good, if fairly austere, life. I don't think being a maths teacher then invigilator until she was 80 was considered sufficient qualification for an obituary, but I disagree. Granny deserves an obituary, so here it is.

Granny Jean (1897 - 1982) ...was the third daughter of a traction engine proprietor, with five younger siblings to follow. She wanted to be a mechanic, to understand how things worked. To her father's eternal credit for a lower middle class Aberdonian in 1914, he said, fine dear, go to University to do physics, and then you can decide. So she went to Aberdeen University. In her first year's exams they called out all the passes but not her name. She worried that she might have failed, but she was singled out for mention for being the first person to ever get 100 percent. Granny liked to get things right. Then the war got in the way a bit, but she finally qualified with a first class honours in Maths and Nat Phil in 1919. She taught maths in Annan where she married Francis in 1940, having two sons, Henry, and five years later, John. She continued to teach the children under the Morrison Table Shelter during the air raids: one can't get little inconveniences like bombs get in the way of a child's education. Francis died suddenly, leaving her with 17 year old Henry and 12 year old John. Within two weeks Granny had sold her house, bought a new one back in her home town, and secured herself a teaching post at Inverurie Academy. She retired at 65, but continued invigilating Highers and O Grades until she was 80.

Henry married Anne and produced three grandchildren, George, Edward and Sophie. My dad married my mum and produced me. Anne and my Mum were decidedly wary of each other for years, until they realised they had both been made to feel totally inadequate by Granny's tales of the marvellous qualities of the other. George and I, six months apart, were also forced into a long distance sibling rivalry by tales of the other's achievements. Granny never quite mastered the art of giving a direct compliment.

Going to Granny's after the fun time with Amah and Ahcong always seemed such a chore, my mum nudging me to say please and thank you (when I was about to say it anyway), with the only noise the tick of the clock and the tiny little rattle of those beads that held down the muslin on the sugar bowl. The floors were highly polished with rugs and a creaky staircase, and it was freezing as soon as you left the sitting room. You could never get your stuff in the wardrobe as it was filled to bursting with exam papers. It was only when I spent a night there without parents, at 18, that I realised Granny was actually a philosopher. I never thought of mathematicians being philosophers, but of course they are: Aristotle, Descartes and Leibniz, the Grandad of optimism, all mathematicians. *Philo = love, Sophia = wisdom.* And my Granny loved wisdom. She was how I imagined Miss Marple to be, except I don't think Miss Marple ever wanted to be a mechanic. And the other thing I discovered was that Granny was human too - she blushed like a girl when I picked up the photo of Grandad Francis and said how handsome he was. But I never saw her again.

After the funeral we went back to Granny's house and I fought with George, Edward and Sophie, over who was to get the last of Granny's special homemade tablet and raspberry cordial. My theory was that it should be split half-half between them and me, but they said that wasn't fair, there were three of them and only one of me, so we should all get a quarter each. They were probably right, but there were only two bottles of raspberry vinegar and they lived in London and I lived in Allanbank, so it just didn't split. Life isn't fair. Did no-one ever tell them? But as grand-children of a mathemetician, we arranged a complicated compromise. Since I have no siblings, I can't go alienating cousins who are actually quite good fun over bottles of raspberry and squares of tablet.

I met a lad at a party at medical school who gasped when he heard my name. He was from Inverurie. "Not any relation to the dreaded 'Mrs. You-may-now-pick-up-your-pencil', are you?" So you see, Granny *was* remembered. And she did make the best tablet and raspberry cordial in the world. Perfect every time.

2. Uncle Henry

Uncle Henry always got bad press from my Mum and Dad. He was deemed boring and English. How would I know, we scarcely ever met? A few times as a child and at the weddings of Granny's grandchildren. I had to give Henry and Anne credit for battling their way up through the snow and ice to our own wedding. Like all the women, I was very impressed with Henry's unexpected lightness of step on the dance floor. (The men had the newly divorced Sophie, his daughter, to impress them). The last time I saw Henry, a few years later, he bounced the gurgly baby Frank on his knee, and actually *enjoyed* playing with Art, who was having one of his maniacal toddler days. My Dad's brother liked children? Surprise, surprise! Like Granny, Uncle Henry was actually okay.

Henry died of lymphoma in his sixties. George made me smile with his eulogy to his Dad. It was weird, like my brother giving a eulogy to my own Dad: George looks like my Dad, he sounds like my Dad, he acts like my Dad and he has the same opinionated stance that should render them both totally obnoxious, but somehow they are both saved by their charm, humour and generosity of spirit.

George described his own Dad, the arch-exponent of rationality, just like mine (well, apart from the liking children and going to church bit). The line ...*such was his delight at his own cleverness, he could hardly ever pass up the opportunity to share them (his awful puns) with us*, had my Dad chuckling in recognition. No wonder the two brothers never saw eye to eye! Granny's sons just liked to be right, like her, like cousin George, like me? (Nah, I'm not nearly as bad as them). *Life is a system of inheritable genetic information...*

Sophie's ex came to Uncle Henry's funeral too, as a gesture of support to Sophie on the death of her beloved Dad. I thought that was nice, and nice too that her new fiancé didn't mind at all. That says a lot for them all.

Anyway, poor old Uncle Henry missed two of his families' best parties that year: his funeral, after the tears had been shed (his children knew they owed their Dad to have a good time) and Sophie's second marriage, in a trendy London bar – just the cure for an unhappy year.

Henry's little brother and his only niece didn't miss either of his parties though, and my Dad and I both agreed that the 'other' side of the family, Urban and English though they may be, could still throw a bloody good party.

3. Mick

It was a relief really. Awful cliché, I'm sorry, and of course he wasn't my son or my brother, but he died peacefully in the end. Or at least the hospice nurses said he did. I don't suppose they'd tell you if it was awful, the actual moment.

Ella being poorly meant I missed most of Mick's funeral. I returned from wheeling Ella round the daffodils to bump into Steve, Mick's son, trying to escape to hide his tears before the end during the closing *You'll Never Walk Alone* (Mick was a Liverpool fan). I'm a little awkward with teenagers, but I hugged the strapping 17 year old, who never really had a mother (well he still did – round the corner in Hedon, but she never came to the funeral, not even for the sake of her son). Mick's stepsons were there though, also weeping for Mick, the best father they had had. The older boys' tears were a much bigger help to Steve than my awkward embrace.

Everyone said it was a good funeral, though. Mick would have been pleased. We all returned to Dee's club for (very early) drinks, sausage rolls and sandwiches. By this time, Ella was back on form (isn't paracetamol wonderful?) and the boys were their usual enthusiastic selves. Children do help at funerals. As long as they're not screaming or vomiting of course.

There were a few funerals I missed altogether.

Five Funerals

1. Ahcong

Ahcong died whilst Danny and I were having a last long weekend in Prague before Art made his appearance. And in typical Scottish style, the funeral was in three days. Relatives made it perfectly well from New York and Geneva but my mum couldn't get hold of us. I would have liked to have gone. I was Ahcong's only granddaughter and his only grandchild for 20 years, and he was the only Granddad I had known. I would liked him to have seen Art, but as Morag, the minister who married us, said at the service – Ahcong did see his first great grandchild, in a scan photo. Ahcong did have an obituary in the Ross-shire journal. And gosh, I never knew he did all that! That was my granddad, you know.

2. Morag

A year later, Morag, Strathfarrell's minister, suddenly collapsed and died. She was in her early fifties. I think I would have liked to go to her funeral too. Morag was kind, generous and fun, the sort of minister who would take a glass of water to an old lady coughing in the congregation during the hymns. She married us, christened Art (and me, belatedly), and was a tower of strength - spiritual, emotional and practical - to Amah, before and after Ahcong's death (personally driving her to the hospital four or five times a week).

3. Aunty Kit

Amah's little sister and everyone's Aunty Kit – although not the postman's. "I'm not your bloody Aunty Kit!" Anyway. Aunty Kit was a wonderful gruff-voiced Katharine Hepburn sort of character and great fun. She lived in Japan, the Congo, Denmark and Geneva, with her husband working with WHO. She was a dentist, but had really wanted to be a vet. She died and was buried without any of us even knowing she was ill. Typical Aunty Kit. Stomach cancer. Bit of a bummer really, as she'd survived ovarian cancer six years earlier (apparently – never told anyone about that either).

4. Phil

I don't usually go to patient's funerals, but I would have liked to have gone to Phil's.

5. Rogie

Cancer. Poor old Rogues had to be put down within a year of leaving us. We had him back at Monikie for a day to say goodbye. Bo woofed at him at first, then they sniffed each others bottoms and settled down in their basket like the old days. I take comfort in the fact Rogie died happy, loved and spoilt to the end by his new family.

Here's my obituary for Rogie:

A beautiful Springer Rogie Nice but Dim,
Bought from the breeders on a whim,
Our pedigree chump,
Was a lovable lump,
And now he's gone, we do miss him.

And that's it, apart from five hamsters, two guinea pigs and two white rats. And thank God, I never had to go to Frankie's funeral.

21.Answers?

Forty Two.

> *"The answer my friend, is blowing in the wind."* Bob Dylan

So what is life all about? Clearly my ability to navel-gaze has vanished with my navel, under a layer of post-natal flab. I've left no brain unpicked: friends, family, philosophers, scientists, writers, psychologists, patients, Baloo the bear and my dog. Oh no, I've forgotten Shakespeare!

> *"All the world's a stage,*
> *And all the men and women merely players:*
> *They have their exits and their entrances;*
> *And one man in his time plays many parts,*
> *His acts being seven ages..."* (*As You Like It*)

That one's for Danny's new-found inner thesp. I can't be upsetting him by missing out Will, the King of Quotes.

Unfortunately my poor friends (mostly under the influence of small children or alcohol) were a bit short of new ideas. But perhaps it's just that the old ones are the best. Aristotle had a hierarchy of needs long before Maslow, and the Chinese had no shortage of one-liner self-help mantras long before Californian Life Coaches. Or even Shakespeare.

> *"He who thinks too much about each step will spend all his life standing on one leg."* Chinese one liner

So here's the top five from my unfocussed focus group. She who has only three pages before the end of her book cannot afford to be fussy.

No. 5 :Life is a fatal sexually transmitted disease

A medical school toilet door classic. And really just a rephrasing of No. 4.

No. 4 : Life is a circle

Perfectly illustrated by one of Yorkshire's favourite songs: *On Ilkley Moor B'a Tat*. We are born and we die, with a varying amount of time in-between, to do a varying amount of things of varying worth, then we are eaten by worms and ingested into the next being. So you can at least take comfort that if you do not achieve quite what you wanted, perhaps some of your organic molecules might make their way into the next Nobel Peace Prize winner, if not in this generation, then at least after another few passages through the cycle. To be a little less optimistic about it, your precious organic molecules could also make their way into the next George Bush or Osama Bin Laden. Of course, George and Osama will also end up eaten by worms, which will in turn be eaten by birds and shat out over the Atlantic (unless of course they are preserved for posterity, either in an urn or in formalin, in which case they'll add nothing at all to future generations.)

No. 3: Life's too short...

"... for chess." Henry James. From Our Boys (1874)

"...to stuff a mushroom." Shirley Conran. From Superwoman (1971)

Of course the Chinese were there first with that idea too:

"Life just gives you time and space, it's up to you to fill it."

My Dad said life is a four letter word. He's right. That word is TIME. Dr. Maslow's (and Aristotle's) basic needs such as eating, breathing, and keeping warm and safe, buy us a bit more time, whereas the higher rung needs are all about the quality of that time. Not everybody wants more time, they would rather be able to do things with the time they have. When age starts to deprive you of your ability to move, hear or even see to read, perhaps time can become a prison.

"...Last scene of all,
That ends this strange eventful history,
Is second childishness, and mere oblivion,
Sans teeth, sans eyes, sans taste, sans everything."
(Shakespeare)

"Only the good die young, what did I do wrong?" Aunty Betty (90)

Poor old Aunty Betty is fed up that her food has become tasteless and she can no longer tend her garden, grow her bulbs, bake her cakes, sew her soft toys or knit her jerseys. She can't even get out to buy her own gin. So yes, I want more time, but I want it now when I can make use of it.

Unfortunately, we just don't get all the time we want. Not like some:

God inhabits eternity. Isaiah 57:15

No. 2: God

The fact that God wasn't number one says something rather worrying about the company I keep, but I can't be massaging my results for a ticket to heaven. I used to be an agnostic but now I'm not so sure.

At the risk of my mother disowning me, here's my argument for believing in God (just to make amends for having Him at number two).

Why would evolution come up with a human? Clever though we may be, we can't photosynthesise, we haven't got big teeth, we can't run very fast, we can't fly, we can't swim underwater, we nearly choke ourselves trying to talk, we have a terrible time in childbirth and we're absolutely helpless as babies. Jews, Christians and Muslims all believe that human life was made in the image of God, and really only God could have come up with such an outrageous concept as a human being. Surely there had to be a higher power to spot our potential amidst all those weaknesses?

Those that believe that Darwin was wrong (www. darwinwaswrong.com) argue that if there are 1.5 million named species (and probably another 30 million un-named) with an estimated evolutionary turnover of a hundred times that, we should have discovered a lot more fossil species than the paltry 250,000 to date. I'm no palaeontologist, but apparently the fossil record doesn't offer much support for gradual change, with all the crucial missing links between blue-green algae and us suspiciously missing. The other side (www.darwinwasright.com) argue that you're much more likely to decompose than fossilize, so it's amazing we've found as many fossils as we have, and besides, there's nothing the scientists love more than mysterious gaps to figure out.

Personally I think the whole thing was an accident ...

Accidental Genesis

"Life is what climbed out of the primordial soup." My Dad

"Evolution's fine, if you've got plenty of time." Colin Thompson, *Fish are So Stupid and Other Poems*

On the first day God was a little bored, sat alone in the void, with all His basic needs met, and He couldn't even entertain Himself musing on the meaning of life, because He knew the answer already, so He started experimenting and whoops! The Universe.

"Oh!" said God, "Fascinating!"

On the second day, God said, let there be 92 elements and let them bump into each other and make ever more complex molecules. On the third day (time is all relative, so let's not get sniffy about a few billion years) He said, let there be the Sun, and let there be planets in its orbit. And God looked at all His stars and His planets and He was pleased. On the fourth day He said, let there be water on that nice looking third planet, and let's make soup! And so He stirred up a few amino acids and zapped it with a few million flashes of lightning and with a bit of luck, whoops, my word, on the fifth day there was a blue-green algae!

3,000 million years later, whoops, a fish! 70 million years later, plants! 40 million years later, an animal! 170 million years after that, a dinosaur! And God liked what He had created, and was pleased.

On the sixth day there was a bit of a disaster, but God is an optimist and optimists don't give up just because their masterpieces have been wiped out. So God thought He'd try something a bit different: something argumentative (just for fun) and capable of love (as really, He wasn't getting much from those cockroaches and the dinosaurs, much as He missed them, were a bit, well, cold), so on the seventh day, 223 million years later, He created woman. And a few minutes later, man. (I'm sorry, forget spare ribs: genetically and embryologically, woman came first). But if there are any men reading this, do not despair. The great thing about being last is that it gives you longer to evolve.

Then two million years later, an hour before midnight on the seventh day, just before the end of the tax year, whoops, Mr. and Mrs. Joy, it's a girl! Me! Honeymoon baby. A happy accident?

God was probably quite excited by project mankind at first, sitting at His great big widescreen 3D multiplex, chortling over all our foibles. "Oh, I don't believe it! What do they think they're doing? Whatever next? Oh, I can't bear to look. Look at that one ...Oh, no she's not going to... oh yes, she is. I don't believe it!!! I'm so glad I gave them the seven deadly sins, it's so much more fun."

A few thousand years later it's just possible that the novelty has worn off. Now He's channel-hopping through the world, trying to find a program with a little less sex and a little less violence and perhaps just a little bit of goodness and happy endings? He must be wondering: "Do I let them sort this almighty mess out themselves, or do I intervene big time and try again with another species that might be a bit more blooming grateful?"

Talking of ingratitude, why wasn't God at number one? Who pipped him to the top spot?

No. 1 (Tum, tum, tum, tum, ta-ta ...): 42. Douglas Adams(1979)

Hmmmm? I doubt that even the Chinese came up with that one (but if anyone knows to the contrary, do let me know.)

This answer is a little less amusing than it once was: the life expectancy in Sierra Leone was 42, Elvis was 42 when he died, and without having to admit my great age, 42 suddenly seems very, very young to die.

Life is a series of accidents never even made it to the top five. Never mind. I'm going to include a definition from one of Douglas Adams' friends, which says the same thing.

"The essence of life is statistical improbability on a colossal scale." Richard Dawkins (1986)

Richard Dawkins, evolutionary biologist and author of *The Selfish Gene* is also president of the British Atheist Association. No doubt he'll be delighted to hear that his pal Doug bumped God off the top spot.

It's probably just as hard to argue with a committed atheist as it is to argue with a fundamentalist Muslim or Christian, and Richard Dawkins is an extremely clever bloke, but clearly with my extensive knowledge of astrophysics, chemistry, biology and palaeontology, I've already proved that there's no reason at all that you can't have an Accidental Almighty. (And I'm still a little anxious about having Him at No. 2.)

If life is a statistical improbability, then isn't God that little spark between probability and what actually happens?

Why can't we have accidents, evolution, statistics, good hard scientific proof, world peace, eternal happiness, unlimited chocolate and God? God could create Life, the Universe and Everything as a living self-sustaining organism, which then takes on a life of its own: beautiful, cruel, and random. Natural disasters are the result of a living universe. God doesn't necessarily make meteorites and tsunamis, just like I don't make my three-year old knock over her third cup of milk. God has to clear up the mess, just like I have to clear up the spilt milk. Fortunately God has a few more tricks and a lot more patience.

Let's take that great big meteorite:

"!@£$%" said God, and God wasn't pleased at all. But optimists don't cry over spilt milk. Life goes on. He looks at the mess and sighs. "Right. How am I going to sort this one out?" And really, that's just what we do (no doubt after a few more !@£$%$£$!s). We are chips off the great big block of life.

Like any offspring, we think ourselves cleverer than our parent. We've messed about with breeding and even cloning, but that's just biogenesis (making life from life), not creating life. The closest we've come was the Ury-Miller experiment in 1957 where with the help of lots of sparks of electricity and some UV light they managed to make a few amino acids in a flask, which are only the barest building blocks of life (but a lot less trouble, I'm sure).

So what will we have? A well-behaved amino acid or a troublesome real live organism?

And what makes us such trouble? All those needs!

Yes Dr. Maslow, it's all your fault. (Phew! I wondered how I was going to get him back in the book). All those needs we have to fulfil just for life to continue, not to mention the luxurious extras on the higher rungs. The most troublesome life-forms of all are those that want to fulfil all their needs, and all their wants too.

"Nothing is enough for the man to whom enough is too little." Epicurus

And we want to be happy!

Life; liberty and the pursuit of happiness. 4th July 1776
Thomas Jefferson et al.

Can you pursue happiness? I suspect it will run away if you do. Most of our needs in the West are met, yet still we are unhappy. Maslow said that if we did not become what we were meant to be we would be unhappy. He said a painter must paint, a writer must write (and, presumably, a bully must pull a small girl's hair?)

Most of us have lots of things we can do, including only some that we actually want to do, rather a lot that we must do whether we want to or not (and some that we probably shouldn't do). We become unhappy if we resent not being able to fulfil every one of our wants, which is clearly impossible. It might be possible to fulfil all of your needs, just not all at the same time. You can't stand on top of Everest and be at home with your family, just as you probably can't have a baby and sleep. If we are grateful for our needs that are met, rather than fretting about the ones that aren't, then we can be happy.

A Tale of Two Pyramids

There are those who have to struggle to meet their basic needs, and those who have their basic needs taken from them. In the midst of a drought in Ethiopia, you have to find water and food, in civil war in Sierra Leone, people did not have food, shelter or safety, in South East Asia after the Tsunami, again, loss of safety, loss of loved ones, loss of their shelters, loss of decent drinking water (further threatening safety), loss of livelihood and thus loss of food.

1) A Sustainable Pyramid

Before diamonds and rebels destroyed Sierra Leone, you could climb to the top of the pyramid pretty simply – even if the life expectancy was only 42. Basic needs? Well food was perhaps not quite to Western tastes, but mashed leaves, dried fish, oil and rice covered all the major food groups. Bananas, oranges and peanuts were available on the side all year round, plus, in season, pineapples, avocado pears, cherry tomatoes and mangoes. Not a bad diet really. Yes, you had to work a bit: growing the rice, the beans, the leaf; pounding the rice to dehusk it and pounding the cassava leaves to get rid of the cyanide, then carrying wood to build the three-stone fire to cook your dinner. Water could be difficult too, but with a bit of effort, a walk to the well, or the river, or rolling a barrel under the corrugated iron roof when it rained, it was possible to get enough, as long as you didn't waste it. Sleep wasn't usually a problem, and you would take a nap in the afternoon when it got too hot. Shelters were simple but effective (of course it was always warm, so perfect draft insulation wasn't necessary). Sex and reproduction could become a problem if the resultant population increase overstretched the system, but did produce a great extended family that fulfilled love and belonging needs, much better than we do in the 'civilised world'. And for the higher needs, there were stories, songs and music, beauty, their own system of justice and morals (most of which was very similar to our own) and plenty of humour, fun and laughter.

What was wrong with that? A sustainable lifestyle over thousands of years.

2) An Overdeveloped Pyramid

Our current Western lifestyle can only be sustainable over a few decades. We are way oversubscribed on basic needs (food and drink in particular) to the point that we are endangering our hearts, joints and liver. Our shelters are larger than we really need, thus needing more fuel to light and heat them, putting us under the stress of work (often miles away, causing more stress and using more fuel) to pay for the mortgage for our overly large shelters, plus the bills to heat them. Then we become guilty at our own excesses. Our sleep is disrupted by overindulgence and staying up too late because we have electric light to do so, or just want to see the end of a film on the telly. Then there is more stress (and fuel) for long distance travel to see extended family and friends, because they no longer live in our village. And because our extended family and friends don't live in our villages, mums are becoming depressed and neurotic, home alone with small babies, whilst elder family members are also home alone with no-one, so they just slowly dement or die.

Is this a better, more civilized, life than the one in Sierra Leone?

Like I said at the start, life comes down to priorities. And just as we all have our own pyramids (fatter, thinner, taller, shorter, basking in the African sun or shivering in British drizzle), we all have our own priorities. And these priorities change as we move through the seven ages of man. Maslow has self-actualisation at the top of his pyramid, what do I have at the top of mine?

Well, at the moment it's a bit crowded: sleep, food, love (physical and emotional), family, peace, to have fun and work. I do need work to feel wanted/needed/useful and, yes, to bring in money, because I do want to be able to afford warmth, shelter and food for my children (and preferably to be able to pay someone to do my cooking, cleaning and ironing because I can't be bothered and never like doing things I am bad at). Is finding out the meaning of life on my list of priorities? Well, no. Life's too random, accidental, wonderful and beautiful. It doesn't need to have meaning to justify itself.

Life really is just a series of accidents. Things go wrong, but then life would never have happened if things didn't go wrong. Embrace those accidents, bad and good - they are life itself. Every accident opens up another possibility.

"There are always possibilities." Mr. Spock, An Unemotional Optimist (2253ish)

I think I'll conclude with Leibniz, the 'founder of optimism'. Rubbish of course; how would we have survived until the seventeenth century if we'd all been pessimists? Anyway. Leibniz:

"Our world is the best of all possible worlds."

So let all those possibilities make your world the best of all possible worlds, even if it's a bit of a mess. And don't forget Baloo.

"Look for the bare necessities, the simple bare necessities, forget about your worries and your strife, yeah man, I mean the bare necessities, that means a bear can rest at ease ...the simple bare necessities of life."

About Eye Books

Eye books is a young, dynamic publishing company that likes to break the rules. Our independence allows us to publish books which challenge the way people see things. It also means that we can offer new authors a platform from which they can shine their light and encourage others to do the same.

To date we have published 30 books that cover a number of genres including Travel, Biography, Adventure and History. Many of our books are experience driven. All of them are inspirational and life-affirming.

Frigid Women, for example, tells the story of the world-record making first all female expedition to the North Pole. A fifty year-old mother of three who had recently recovered from a mastectomy, and her daughter are the authors neither had ever written a book before. Sue Riches is now both author and highly sought after motivational speaker.

We also publish thematic anthologies, such as The Tales from Heaven and Hell series, for those who prefer the short story format. Here everyone has the chance to get their stories published and win prizes such as flights to any destination in the world.

And here's what makes us really different: As well as publishing books, Eye Books has set up a club for like-minded people and is in the process of developing a number of initiatives and services for its community of members. After all, the more you put into life, the more you get out of it.

Please visit www.eye-books.com for further information.

New Titles

Riding the Outlaw Trail - Simon Casson
A true story of an epic horseback journey by two Englishmen from Mexico to Canada, across 2,000 miles of some of America's most difficult terrain. Their objective? To retrace the footsteps of those legendary real life bandits Butch Cassidy and the Sundance Kid, by riding the outlaw trails they rode more than a century ago.
ISBN: 1 903070 228. Price £9.99.

Desert Governess - Phyllis Ellis
Phyllis, a former Benny Hill actress, takes on a new challenge when she becomes a governess to the Saudi Arabian Royal family. In this frank personal memoir, she gives us an insider's view into the Royal family and a woman's role in this mysterious kingdom.
ISBN: 1 903070 015. Price £9.99.

Last of the Nomads - W. J. Peasley
Warri and Yatungka were the last of the desert nomads to live permanently in the traditional way. Their deaths marked the end of a tribal lifestyle that stretched back more than 30,000 years. The Last of the Nomads tells of an extraordinary journey in search of Warri and Yatungka, their rescue and how they survived alone for thirty years in the unrelenting Western Desert region of Australia.
ISBN: 1 903070 325. Price £9.99.

All Will Be Well - Michael Meegan
So many self help books look internally to provide inspiration, however this book looks at how love and compassion when given out to others, can act as a better antidote to the human condition than trying to inwardly solve feelings of discontentment.
ISBN: 1 903070 279. Price £9.99.

First Contact - Mark Anstice

This is a true story of a modern day exploration by two young adventurers and the discovery of cannibal tribes in the 21st century. An expedition far more extraordinary than they had ever imagined, one that would stretch them, their friendship and their equipment to the limits.

ISBN: 1 903070 260. Price £9.99.

Further Travellers' Tales From Heaven and Hell - Various

This is the third book in the series, after the first two best selling Travellers' Tales from Heaven and Hell. It is an eclectic collection of over a hundred anecdotal travel stories which will enchant you, shock you and leave you in fits of laughter!

ISBN: 1 903070 112. Price £9.99.

Special Offa - Bob Bibby

Following his last best selling book Dancing with Sabrina, Bob walks the length of Offa's Dyke. He takes us through the towns and villages that have sprung up close by and reveals their ancient secrets and folklore. He samples the modern day with his refreshingly simple needs and throws light on where to go and what to see.

ISBN: 1 903070 287. Price £9.99.

The Good Life - Dorian Amos

Needing a change and some adventure, Dorian and his wife searched their world atlas and decided to sell up and move to Canada. Having bought Pricey the car, Boris Lock their faithful dog, a canoe and their fishing equipment they set off into the Yukon Wilderness to find a place they could call home.

ISBN: 1 903070 309. Price £9.99.

Baghdad Business School - Heyrick Bond Gunning
A camp bed, ten cans of baked beans, some water and $25,000
is all that was needed to set up an International Business in Iraq.
The book chronicles an amusing description of the trials and
tribulations of doing business in an environment where explosions
and shootings are part of everyday life, giving the reader a unique
insight into what is really happening in this country.
ISBN: 1 903070 333. Price £9.99.

Green Oranges on Lion Mountain - Emily Joy
Armed with a beginner's guide to surgery, GP Emily Joy took up
her VSO posting at a remote hospital in Sierra Leone. As she set off
into the unknown, action, adventure and romance were high on
her agenda; rebel forces and the threat of civil war were not.
ISBN: 1 903070 295. Price £9.99.

Also available as an audiobook:
ISBN: 1 903070 465. Price £9.99

The Con Artist Handbook - Joel Levy
Get wise with The Con Artist's Handbook as it blows the lid
on the secrets of the successful con artist and his con games.
Get inside the hustler's head and find out what makes him tick;
Learn how the world's most infamous scams are set up and
performed; Peruse the career profiles of the most notorious
scammers and hustlers of all time; Learn to avoid the modern-
day cons of the e-mail and Internet age.
ISBN: 1 903070 341. Price £9.99.

Zohra's Ladder - Pamela Windo
Pamela spent seven years living in Morocco and recalls a
selection of tales that immerses the reader in a world of ritual
and deep sensuality. She peels back layers of history and finely
embroidered fabric of everyday life to find the truths in the
mysterious and exotic.
ISBN: 1 903070 406. Price £9.99

The Forensics Handbook - Pete Moore

The Forensic Handbook is the most up-to-date log of forensic techniques available. Discover how the crime scene is examined using examples of some of the most baffling crimes; Learn techniques of lifting and identifying prints; Calculate how to examine blood splatter patterns; Know what to look for when examining explosive deposits, especially when terrorist activity is suspected. Learn how the Internet is used to trace stalkers.

ISBN: 1 903070 35X. Price £9.99.

My Journey With A Remarkable Tree - Ken Finn

Ken set out exploring Cambodia to indulge his passion and fascination with trees. What he found was certainly moving but in a much bleaker way than he had ever imagined. His journey became a mission as he followed his once remarkable tree from spirit forest to the furniture corner of a garden centre.

ISBN: 1 903070 384. Price £9.99

Seeking Sanctuary - Hilda Reilly

Seeking Sanctuary tells the stories of a group of Muslim converts from the west who found liberation in Sudan. They describe their spiritual and physical journeys from one way of life to another. And they gift us insights that challenge lazy prejudice about Islam by providing a striking counterpoint to fears about fundamentalism, extremism, and religious hostility.

ISBN: 1 903070 392. Price £9.99

Lost Lands Forgotten Stories - Alexandra Pratt

Inspired by Mina Hubbard who made an astonishing 600 mile river journey in 1905 to restore the reputation of her late husband who had died on the same route, Alexandra Pratt retraces Hubbard's steps through the wild and ancient land of Labrador as she confronts an unforgiving landscape that surprises her at every turn.

ISBN: 1 903070 368. Price £9.99

Also by Eye Books

Jasmine and Arnica - Nicola Naylor
A blind woman's journey around India.
ISBN: 1 903070 171. Price £9.99.

Touching Tibet - Niema Ash
A journey into the heart of this intriguing forbidden kingdom.
ISBN: 1 903070 18X. Price £9.99.

Behind the Veil - Lydia Laube
A shocking account of a nurses Arabian nightmare.
ISBN: 1 903070 198. Price £9.99.

Walking Away - Charlotte Metcalf
A well known film makers African journal.
ISBN: 1 903070 201. Price £9.99.

Travels in Outback Australia - Andrew Stevenson
In search of the original Australians - the Aboriginal People.
ISBN: 1 903070 147. Price £9.99

The European Job - Jonathan Booth
10,000 miles around Europe in a 25 year old classic car.
ISBN: 1 903070 252. Price £9.99

Around the World with 1000 Birds - Russell Boyman
An extraordinary answer to a mid-life crisis.
ISBN: 1 903070 163. Price £9.99

Cry from the Highest Mountain - Tess Burrows
A climb to the point furthest from the centre of the earth.
ISBN: 1 903070 120. Price £9.99

Dancing with Sabrina - Bob Bibby
A journey from source to sea of the River Severn.
ISBN: 1 903070 244. Price £9.99

Grey Paes and Bacon - Bob Bibby
A journey around the canals of the Black Country
ISBN: 1 903070 066. Price £7.99

Jungle Janes - Peter Burden
Twelve middle-aged women take on the Jungle. As seen on Ch 4.
ISBN: 1 903070 05 8. Price £7.99

Travels with my Daughter - Niema Ash
Forget convention, follow your instincts.
ISBN: 1 903070 04 X. Price £7.99

Riding with Ghosts - Gwen Maka
One woman's solo cycle ride from Seattle to Mexico.
ISBN: 1 903070 00 7. Price £7.99

Riding with Ghosts: South of the Border - Gwen Maka
The second part of Gwen's epic cycle trip across the Americas.
ISBN: 1 903070 09 0. Price £7.99

Triumph Round the World - Robbie Marshall
He gave up his world for the freedom of the road.
ISBN: 1 903070 08 2. Price £7.99

Fever Trees of Borneo - Mark Eveleigh
A daring expedition through uncharted jungle.
ISBN: 0 953057 56 9. Price £7.99

Discovery Road - Tim Garrett and Andy Brown
Their mission was to mountain bike around the world.
ISBN: 0 953057 53 4. Price £7.99

Frigid Women - Sue and Victoria Riches
The first all-female expedition to the North Pole.
ISBN: 0 953057 52 6. Price £7.99

Jungle Beat - Roy Follows
Fighting Terrorists in Malaya.
ISBN: 0 953057 57 7. Price £7.99

Slow Winter - Alex Hickman
A personal quest against the backdrop of the war-torn Balkans.
ISBN: 0 953057 58 5. Price £7.99

Tea for Two - Polly Benge
She cycled around India to test her love.
ISBN: 0 953057 59 3. Price £7.99

Traveller's Tales from Heaven and Hell - Various
A collection of short stories from a nationwide competition.
ISBN: 0 953057 51 8. Price £6.99

More Traveller's Tales from Heaven and Hell - Various
The second collection of short stories.
ISBN: 1 903070 02 3. Price £6.99

A Trail of Visions: Route 1 - Vicki Couchman
A stunning photographic essay.
ISBN: 1 871349 338. Price £14.99

A Trail of Visions: Route 2 - Vicki Couchman
The second stunning photographic essay.
ISBN: 0 953057 50 X. Price £16.99

Book Microsites

If you are interested in finding out more about this book please visit our book microsite:

www.eye-books.com/firstcontact/home.htm

We have also created microsites for a number of our other new books including:

Riding The Outlaw Trail
Desert Governess
The Last of the Nomads
First Contact
Special Offa
The Good Life
Green Oranges on Lion Mountain
Baghdad Business School

For details on these sites and others which we are developing please visit our main website:

www.eye-books.com

Special Offers and Promotions

We are offering our club members and people who have read this book the opportunity to take advantage of promotions on our other books by buying direct from us.

For information on these special offers please visit the following page of our website:

www.eye-books.com/promotions.htm